THIS
Book
IS a
gift

From

_____

To

_____

On the Occasion of

_____

Date

_____

DR. ABRAHAM CHIGBUNDU

MYSTERIES OF THE ALTARS

MYSTERIES OF THE ALTARS

Unless otherwise indicated, all scriptural references are from the New King James Version of the Holy Bible.

Please note we capitalize certain pronouns in Scripture that refer to the Father, Son, and Holy Spirit, and may differ from some Bible publisher's style. Take note also that the name satan and related names are not capitalized. We choose not to acknowledge him, even to the point of violating grammatical rules.

PUBLISHED IN NIGERIA BY:

FREEDOM PUBLICATIONS
21, Adesuwa Grammar School Road, GRA.
P.O.BOX 7240, Benin City, Nigeria.
Tel: 08022908737, 08023381077
Email: bishopchigbundu@gmail.com
Website: www.voiceoffreedomonline.com

EDITING, DESIGN & PRINTS:
Aaron & Hur Publishing (*A member of the BSA Group*)
16, Thomas Salako Street, Ogba-Ikeja, Lagos-Nigeria.
21-25, Hanover Street, Kingston CSO. Jamaica.WI
T: 0703 512 1346, 0809 703 2664, + 1 (876) 286 3343
E: info@aaronandhurpublishing.com
W: www.aaronandhurpublishing.com

Table of Contents

Dedication

This book is dedicated to my darling wife, Rev (Mrs.)
Florence Chigbundu, my jewel of inestimable value. It
is also dedicated to my lovely children, Emmanuel,
Faith, Mike and David, you all are sources of inspiration
to me.

Acknowledgements

If you want to travel fast, travel alone, but if you want to travel far, travel with people.

I wish to thank my daughter Pastor Anthonia Innocent for her great inputs in editing this work. God richly bless you.

Also worthy of mention is Basola Victor and his team at Aaron & Hur Publishing, Lagos for their passion and creativity in the production of this book.

May God richly reward all of you in Jesus name. Amen.

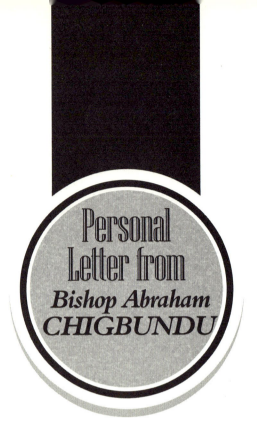

Personal Letter from *Bishop Abraham* CHIGBUNDU

Dear reader,

There is no such thing as coincidence. Nothing happens just by chance. This planet is intelligently governed both physically and spiritually. Everything you see happening is directly or indirectly traceable to an influence and that is clearly because the spiritual controls the physical.

Also, the physical resembles the spiritual. Everything that will ever happen on earth has first been concluded in the realms of the spirit.

This is where this book in your hands comes to play. I am with this book introducing you to the mysteries of the altars. This is a much neglected area of spiritual warfare amongst many believers. The resultant effect of this neglect has cost many children of God their inheritances in Christ.

You are about to learn and have a full understanding of the power behind the altars and how it has shaped God's dealings with man through the ages and into our present times. You will also discover how satan has seized this same truth and perverted it to advance his own agenda, thereby putting many generations in unfortunate circumstances, evil cycles and strange happenings.

Some people are today facing untold hardships not because God has forgotten them or because God has changed but simply because an altar was raised decades or centuries before they were born and they are not knowledgeable about it.

However, on the flip side of the coin, many believers are presently reclaiming their lost blessings simply because they have come to understand the dynamic mysteries of the Altar available in Christ.

I hope this book gets you angry – angry enough to fight in fervent and aggressive prayers till you take back everything the enemy of your destiny has stolen from you.

May your eyes of understanding be opened as I walk you through this life changing adventure on the mysteries of the altars. It is your turn to share a testimony.

Yours in the Master's Service

Bishop Dr. Abraham Chigbundu
Benin, Nigeria

CHAPTER 1

UNDERSTANDING
THE ALTARS

An altar is a spiritual system which controls human destinies through sacrifices and words.

UNDERSTANDING THE ALTARS

And Noah builded an altar unto the LORD; and took of every clean beast, and of every clean fowl, and offered burnt offerings on the altar. And the LORD smelled a sweet savour; and the LORD said in his heart, I will not again curse the ground any more for man's sake; for the imagination of man's heart is evil from his youth; neither will I again smite any more everything living, as I have done. While the earth remaineth, seedtime and harvest, and cold and heat, and summer and winter, and day and night shall not cease.
Gen 8:20-22

Interestingly, as the human race advances more towards modernization, there is a tendency to disregard and belittle the concept of the ALTAR. Those who lived in ancient and medieval times clearly understood the importance and impact of the altar. Thank God we have the Bible which is a book from the past influencing the present, determining and concluding the future.

Those who lived in the Biblical times clearly understood

the concept of the altar. They were people who lived in the areas we know today as the Middle East and North Africa.

In the ancient times and presently, in the continent of Africa, this concept is still very much in use and also very active. No person of African descent should disregard this issue because Africans all come from a common lineage, village, clan, bloodline or family tree that have at one time or the other operated the principles and procedures of altars. It is therefore very important to take this matter very seriously.

IGNORANCE IS VERY COSTLY

What you do not understand can cost you dearly. In fact, what you do not know can cause you a colossal loss and even lead to death. Ignorance is never an excuse in the court of law and more importantly, not on this battlefield called life. One cannot afford to be slack! It is time to brace up and get informed.

> *My people are destroyed for lack of knowledge: because thou hast rejected knowledge, I will also reject thee, that thou shalt be no priest to me: seeing thou hast forgotten the law of thy God, I will also forget thy children. Hosea 4:6*

Can I tell you the truth? The field of ignorance is where the enemy wants you to remain so he can continue to steal your virtues, kill your dreams and destroy your life unchallenged and uninterrupted?

> *Therefore my people are gone into captivity, because they have no knowledge: and their honourable men are famished, and their multitude dried up with thirst. Isaiah 5:13*

You cannot intelligently confront what you don't understand. Your enemy is more formidable if you have no information about his strength, warfare strategies, the size of his army and his weapons of war.

The ignorance of the oppressed is the strength of the oppressor. It is therefore important that we understand by definitions what I mean by the mysteries of the altars.

WHAT IS A MYSTERY

A mystery is a hidden fact of truth that can only be known by revelation. In other words, you may never lay hold on it unless you are helped to grasp its reality in your mind by divine insight.

Mysteries are secrets or hidden truths knowable by divine revelations. Mysteries are responsible for miseries or miracles. Divine mysteries will produce miracles while demonic mysteries will produce miseries.

A mystery is a hidden truth encapsulated by hard sentences and codes that can only be deciphered by privileged insight. If you don't know it, you don't know it.

It cannot be taught, it can only be unveiled. A mystery is also a code of information not accessible to the ordinary man. A mystery is the basis upon which many occurrences come to bear upon humanity. God is a God of mysteries. He is Himself a mysterious God. This is why Jesus spoke about the mysteries of the kingdom of God in **Mark 4:11**.

> *And he said unto them, Unto you it is given to know the MYSTERY OF THE KINGDOM OF GOD: but unto them that are without, all these things are done in parables. Mark 4:11*

The kingdom of God is governed by mysteries. God can only be discovered and encountered by revelation; you can never understand God by head knowledge. Also, because of the ability of men to become familiar with the ordinary, God has hidden himself from men except to those who seek earnestly and search for him diligently with all of their heart.

Apostle Paul also explains the mystery of godliness. This clearly reveals that God works through mysteries. When you follow His mystery, it produces miracle.

The devil is a master when it comes to copying anything that is working. It pains me when I see the children of God refuse to imitate God in their dealings whereas the kingdom of darkness pattern their operations after God's and it is working for them.

Like I said earlier, satan has copied the workings of mysteries from God and he also has mysteries by which he operates. The Bible speaks of the mystery of iniquity in **2 Thessalonians 2:7**. Satan's mysteries, when followed, will end a man in misery.

> *For the mystery of iniquity doth already work: only he who now letteth will let, until he be taken out of the way. 2 Thess 2:7*

ALTARS

Let us take a look at the definitions of Altar. This will help to make you gain understanding of the mystery I am talking about. The word altar and altars are mentioned 374 times in the Bible.

> *How that by revelation he made known unto me the mystery; (as I wrote afore in few words, Whereby, when ye read, ye may understand my knowledge in the mystery of Christ) Eph 3:3-4*

An Altar is a spiritual system with enormous power, which empowers ordinary men with superior authority over other men and other powers in a given territory.

An altar is a spiritual location and meeting place between spirits and mortals where human destinies are decided and altered via the use of sacrifices and spoken words. An altar is a spiritual force that repositions humans to partake of God's abilities (or satan's abilities) to speak/command things which were not into existence.

An altar is a point of spiritual transaction where vital resources are traded between the unseen and the seen realms- and between their representations and representatives.

An Altar is a spiritual gateway of access through which mortal and immortal transit with the purpose of gaining legal relationship and perceived benefits. An altar is a place of interaction and negotiation between humans, spirits and disembodied spirits. Altar is a point of spiritual traffic for the ascending and descending of spirit beings on the basis of covenant enactment.

An Altar is a place of exchange and also a place of change. This point is very profound. Selah! Whether Exchange – positive or negative and change – positive or negatives. (Pause and think please!)

Beloved, this is a very crucial matter. In my teaching, I will give you an over view of the potency of God's altar before my emphasis which is on evil or satanic altars. This is because without the backing of God's altar, your life can be altered on satanic altars.

God's altar in the Bible days was God's presence on earth. Men of old knew the power of God's presence with them in any situation. They knew that their conquest of any territory was by the altar hence when they arrive at any new territory, they will build an altar for God first, because they knew that to win the battles of life and conquer their enemies God's altar must be involved.

The Ark of covenant was an altar to the Israelites in all their wars. It was God's presence with them. Contrary to the beliefs of any people, the new covenant did not change the order rather, it gave us a clearer understanding of the eternal altar where the lamb of God -Jesus was slain before the foundation of the world.

> *And they overcame him by the blood of the Lamb,*
> *and by the word of their testimony; and they loved*
> *not their lives unto the death. Rev 12:11*

Jesus is now the high priest who ministers on the eternal altar daily on behalf of the redeemed. He is the mediator between us and God. Heb.12:11; 1Tim.2:5

> *And to Jesus the mediator of the new covenant, and*
> *to the blood of sprinkling, that speaketh better things*
> *than that of Abel. Heb 12:24*

Understanding of the mystery of that eternal altar is what gives us victory over the counterfeit altar of satan. The devil is a perfect counterfeit producer and knows the mystery of the altar and has taken full advantage of it because of the ignorance of the church. He been a spirit being knows he has no legal authority to operate on planet earth without blood.

He knows that the access to God in the Old Testament was by the blood on the altar. He knows that his defeat was by the blood of Jesus on the cross. He knows that the access to God in the New Testament is also by the blood. So he decided to use humans to produce blood for him on different altars for manipulations of human destinies. The Hebrew word for Altar is: MIZBE-AH which means a place of slaughter while the Greek word for Altar is: TUZIASTERON which means a place of HOLOCAUST---mass slaughter or reckless destruction of life.

It therefore means that an altar is a place where animals or lives are slaughtered or sacrificed to God or deities. Amazingly, it is also where enemies of your destinies are slaughtered. Also it is where marriages, businesses, professions, academics, health's, fortunes and lives are slaughtered.

An altar is a spiritual system which controls human destinies through sacrifices and words. If it is God's altar, destinies are projected to manifestation by the spirit of God. If it is satanic altars, destinies are manipulated to ruin by witchcraft spirits. An altar is a spiritual mystery that empowers an ordinary man with authority over other men, powers and circumstances.

Altar is a spiritual force that empowers humans to partake of God's abilities to speak things into existence. Every priest who ministers on the altar speaks on behalf of the God of the altar. An altar is a translating force that moves a man from the physical realm to the spiritual realm. It gives you access to the invisible power of God. An altar is a place of change and exchange. At salvation, the eternal altar of God with the blood of Jesus spoke and a change took place immediately and your old life was exchanged with a new life. On satanic altars, many destinies have been changed and exchanged. Prosperity was exchanged with poverty, fruitfulness exchanged for barrenness, longevity for untimely death.

Every altar has power behind it which is activated by sacrifice and words (prayer, incantations or enchantments.) Elijah and the prophets of Baal had to erect altars and place sacrifice on it to activate the powers behind the altars by words. (1 Kings 18:25-40)

Every altar has a priest that ministers on it by speaking to the devotees and also on their behalf.

> *But this man, because he continueth ever, hath an unchangeable priesthood. Wherefore he is able also to save them to the uttermost that come unto God by him, seeing he ever liveth to make intercession for them. Heb 7:24-25*

Altars speak. The voice of the altar is the blood which is life.
> *For the life of the flesh is in the blood: and I have given it to you upon the altar to make an atonement for your souls: for it is the blood that maketh an atonement for the soul. Levi. 17:11*

The blood has voice. God's altar with the eternal blood of Jesus speaks better things.
> *And he said, What hast thou done? the voice of thy*

brother's blood crieth unto me from the ground.
Gen 4:10

It speaks success, prosperity, longevity, divine health, greatness. While satanic altars with blood of different animals and humans speaks poverty, failure, sickness, rejection, backwardness, untimely death etc. Where ever you find yourself in life depends on your understanding of the power of the altar speaking on your behalf.

Altar is a raised or designated place where humanity meets with divinity, or deity to cut a covenant.

In Gen. 15:13-21 God made covenant with Abraham to give the land of the Canaanites, Jebusites and other nations to Abraham's seed making a total of 10 nations.

Three Mysteries on this Altar:

(1) A generation's inheritance has been given to an unborn generation without their knowledge.

(2) An unborn generation has been covenanted to an inheritance before they were born.

(3) An unborn generation has been sentenced to a life of miseries without their knowledge.

The implication here is that, upon the altar, a generation's inheritance can be taken and handed over to another by their ancestors without their knowledge.

Unborn generations can be covenanted to inherit what they do not know its origin.

Some people's inheritance has been handed over to other people without their knowledge. The ten nations did not know that their inheritance have been handed over to another nation until many generations after. It was a surprise to a new generation of Canaanites when Joshua came and took their land from them.

Many people have lost so much in life because their ancestors sold their inheritance before they were born. Abraham accepted that his seed will go into bondage for 400yrs. He had opportunity to plead for a change or reduction of the years but did not.

It is pertinent to note that Abraham entered into this covenant but he did not experience it. The exchange for possessing the land was 400years of slavery in a strange land. In every covenant something is exchanged. That means something is taken and given. Mysteriously, those who entered into a covenant are not the ones that experience the outcome but a generation that did not know of it.

If you don't raise a strong altar for yourself, the altars of your ancestors will continue to hinder and limit your life. It is their altars that have stagnated you and if you must move from where they kept you, you must as a matter of urgency raise your own altar with a great and painful sacrifice. Mind you that their altars have received sacrifices for many years.

The Altar is a place where scarifies are offered to God or deities in worship, for intervention or vengeance. The Altar is a place where destines are projected to manifest or hijacked through the instrumentality of sacrifice and words. Altar is a place where covenants and dedications that promote or ruin destinies are made.

Altar is the foundation of all generational blessings, curses and issues. An Altar is the entry point of demonic powers into families and communities. All demonic powers in families, communities, cities and nations have their access route through the altars.

An Altar is where blessings or curses are established. Abraham obtained blessing for his generation on the altar while Ahab obtained curses for his children on the altar of Baal. Altars are where mysteries behind miracles or miseries are established. An Altar is your strongest weapon in spiritual warfare if you understand its importance and activate it accordingly.

An Altar is the strongest stronghold in your life because of your ignorance and because of the power of incantations, curses, enchantments covenants and dedications sealed with much sacrifices from the past.

There are human altars, men and women who have developed constant and unbroken covenant with God. They speak as God. An encounter with them can change your life forever. Moses laid hand on Joshua, spoke and changed his destiny. Elisha spoke into Gehazi and altered his life including his seed. Samuel anointed

David and Saul and changed their lives. In the same vein there are human satanic altars. Any contact with them can ruin your destiny just like Delilah ruined Samson's ministry and caused him untimely death. I have seen many who have had sexual contact with such human altars and their destinies crumbled.

CHAPTER

2

ALTARS AND
DISPENSATIONS

If you don't raise a strong altar for yourself, the altars of your ancestors will continue to hinder and limit your life.

2

ALTARS AND DISPENSATIONS

God is a God of dimensions and dispensations. Since, He is the originator of the concept of raising altars; it therefore means that He brings for the operation of the altar in several dimensions and in diverse dispensations.

We will be taking a look at the altar as it pertains to some various dimensions and at different dispensations revealed in the Bible. This will be examined based on some key Bible characters in scriptures. These are persons who engage the mystery of the altars in the carrying out of their divine assignments' from God.

Abraham

We begin with Abraham, the Friend of God. From the beginning of his friendship with God when He was first called in Genesis 12:1-3, we see a man who was quick to understand the importance of raising an altar of sacrifice to God at every point in time.

God was so fond of Abraham that He had to admit that

He could not do anything without first checking out on Abraham's opinion on the matter. Genesis 18:17

Abraham was God's confidant. He was God's pal. As a matter of fact, it would interest you to know that the only other person in Heaven called "Father" besides God Almighty is Abraham. And anytime Abraham is called "father", God does not feel jealous! What an amazing man he must be! Even in hell, Abraham's fatherhood is saluted. Luke 16: 22-24

Furthermore, the Bible makes mention of a place called Abraham's bosom, where the departed souls of the saints abode temporarily. Whenever God wants to do a major thing, He refers you back to His dealings with Abraham. That is what He meant in Isaiah 51:1-3. In the following scriptures, we see how Abraham would raise altars of sacrifice as he entered a new place. Genesis 12 & 13.

Then in Genesis 22:1-19, he was instructed by God to raise an altar but this time, Isaac the son whom he had waited for about twenty five years to get was to be the sacrifice. The powerful sacrifice brought Abraham's relationship with God into the dimension of what I call "Sworn Blessings". (Genesis 22:1)

God was so moved by Abraham's faith of raising an altar of sacrifice with Isaac that he swore by Himself since there was none else greater than Him. This is a powerful revelation here.

There are various dimensions of divine blessings. There

are promised blessings. Anybody can get the promised blessings so long as you faithfully keep to the principles of God in the area of life you seek an answer.

But then, there is a higher dimension that is greater than the promised blessing. It is called the sworn blessing. At this point, God will swear an oath to bless you on a trans-generational dimension. Such a blessing will transcend your days. No enemy can raise an altar to defeat a believer who has raised the Abrahamic kind of altar of sworn blessings. Abrahamic walk with God introduces us to that dimension of giving or sacrificing the most precious on the altar. Heaven can never pretend to not see the man who raises the sworn blessing provocative altar. Hebrews 6:13-17

This dimension of altar in the kingdom makes God to enter into an oath with the believer. God is calling for believers who are willing to enter into this frequency of the altars with Him. At this point, God takes ownership of your battles. Psalm 50:4, Hebrews 6:13-17

When life's biggest battles rise against you, it is time to raise the sacrificial altar of sworn blessings. You will never record a loss in battle again in Jesus name!

Noah

The man called Noah was a man whose life leaves you in awe. This was the man with whom God entrusted the preservation of the human race while he destroyed the then wicked population of the human race in that generation. Noah can be awarded as the greatest short term pastor that ever lived. How can you live under the same roof with wild beasts in a wooden ship drifting to anywhere? The Lion killed no other animal; the snake never used its venom etc. - One man pastored them all!

Noah found favour with God. He lived a righteous life; a very rare thing during the age of unbearable wickedness. God decided to destroy the world's population in the flood.

After the flood was gone from the face of the earth, Noah came out with his family and all the animals. Then he sacrificed the male specie of every clean beast on the first altar that was raised after the flood. How can you sacrifice one out of a male and female pair (because the Bible says: each animal species was paired male and female), and yet after the sacrifice, none of these animals lacked his or her mate. Only God can fully explain that. It was a mysterious altar on Mount Ararat. God was provoked by Noah's act of unparalleled faith by raising such an altar that God still went ahead to provide each animal's specie with either a replacement or raised a new version- I do not know how God did it. That is why He alone is God!

Isaiah 34: 16, the Bible says "none shall want her mate".

It was a risky sacrifice. Sometimes God seeks believers who can raise a "risky" sacrificial seed on the altar before Him. The result will be similar to what transpired in

Noah's time. God spoke a covenant vowing never again to destroy the world. Such an altar will put an end or a final stop to any attempt by the wicked to make afflictions rise again. *Genesis 8: 15-22*

The Altar of Noah provoked the Almighty God to establish the comforting sign of the rainbow for all generations assuring us that destruction of that kind would never happen again.

When you raise an altar such as Noah's, i.e. an altar with a very seemingly risky sacrificial seed, you can expect God to give a great miraculous sign of a colourful testimony. God will colour your life for all coming generations to see that He is your God. God will beautify the heavens over your head with a colourful testimony in Jesus name. *Genesis 9:11-17*

If you will let God smell a sweet savour from an exalted altar of sacrifice such as Noah's, expect God to give you such blessing that adds colours to your life, family, career and destiny.

Joshua

Joshua's story in the Bible is very noteworthy in our discussions of raising the kind of mysterious altar that attracts results from God. He was the man who successfully commanded the sun to stand still, led an army of soldiers and choristers who shouted down the walls of Jericho, and ultimately conquered the heathen occupants of God's land of promise and divided the lands to the Israelite tribes for inheritance. He rose from being Moses' servant to becoming one of the greatest war generals Israel ever had.

This personal assistant-turned-warlord understood the mysteries and power behind raising altars. His is a remarkable life story.

Joshua, after inheriting the leadership position from Moses, received an instruction from God to make the people of Israel perform the circumcision rites again. The male children born during the wilderness journey were yet to be circumcised according to God's instruction given to Abraham several generations prior to Joshua's day. (Genesis 15: 9 – 11)

In Genesis 17, Abraham performed the circumcision rite on himself and on every male child born in his household. Abraham performed this painful ritual after he had already raised an altar with sacrifices of different kinds of animals – a heifer, a goat, a ram, a dove, a young pigeon.

And it came to pass, when all the kings of the Amorites, which were on the side of Jordan westward, and all the kings of the Canaanites, which were by the sea, heard that the LORD had dried up the waters of Jordan from before the children of Israel, until we were passed over, that their heart melted, neither was there spirit in them any more, because of the children of Israel. At that time the LORD said unto Joshua, Make thee sharp knives, and circumcise again the children of Israel the second time. And Joshua made him sharp knives, and circumcised the children of Israel at the hill of the foreskins. *Joshua 5:1-3*

Joshua understood that before starting out in military engagement with his enemies, he must first of all return to the covenant Altar of God with Abraham. He reconnected with what God had arranged with Abraham on the Altar of the circumcision. This set the spiritual platform for victory as he entered the land of promise. I believe that Joshua would not have performed the circumcision without first raising the altar of sacrifices, just as Abraham had done in his days, in Genesis 15: 9-11 and later Genesis 17, Joshua is sure to have followed the order laid down by Abraham. Joshua was a type of Jesus today.

Even Jesus as a baby was circumcised when his parents, Joseph and Mary, had offered the sacrifices for the male child. Luke 1: 21 -24, 27

When you find yourself in the beginning of warfare and spiritual military engagement, then know that it is time to first of all raise a vital altar before the Lord.

In the kingdom of God, spiritual battling does not only start at the prayer ground, it also begins on the altar ground. Your enemy has started his battles against you at the altar of sacrifices; therefore you too, should begin your own military engagement by raising an Altar for victory on the prayer ground. Go a step ahead of your adversaries. Learn to follow Joshua's wisdom by beginning your fight at the altar of sacrifice first.

Moses

Moses is probably the most revered prophet of the Old Testament. He alone, it was recorded, caught a glimpse of the form of God on a mountain. He walked with God in such a manner that leaves many saints wishing they had just a fraction of what he enjoyed with God.

After fleeing Egypt for fear of being killed by pharaoh, Moses spent forty years away from his own people, the enslaved Israelites. Then God appeared to him with a mandate to deliver His enslaved people. None of the miraculous signs and plagues done by Moses could make pharaoh succumb; none could humble the gods of Egypt and their wicked altars.

God delivered into the hand of Moses a formidable spiritual strategy to turn the door posts of the every Israelite's house to an Altar of sacrifice by placing the Blood of the Lamb on the lamp post at the entrance to their homes.

The day after the Passover night (the night when the death angel would inflict vengeance upon Egypt' gods by killing their first born sons), every Israelite stepped over the Blood of the sacrificed Lamb that had dripped over the night. They stepped over a pool of Blood sacrifice and crossed over from a four hundred and thirty year old slavery into an unending season of deliverance. Now, they could walk in the dignity of liberty with a spring in their steps and with their heads held high.

Maybe your family has been in bondage to the evil grip of the altar of slavery. Whatever form of enslavement e.g. financial, martial, health, spiritual, etc.; Moses' story revealed a major secret to real household deliverance. Each household of Israel turned their entrances into an altar. You can deliver your household by raising a family altar of sacrifice. This is key to family deliverance. Add this to all the family prayers you have been engaged in. If it set the enslaved household of Israel free; it will also set your household free.

David

No other king of Israel stands out like David. God called him a man after His own Heart. King David was the only one with a covenant with God concerning having a predecessor on his throne. He alone has spiritual keys of the kingdom named after him- the Keys of David. Such is the greatness placed upon him by God. But then, success can make you behave like a wild beast if you fail to tame yourself and be humble.

In his greatness as king, he made a very costly mistake which wasted the life of seventy thousand innocent people. David counted the people of Israel contrary to the will of God for him. (2 Samuel 24:1)

The real error here was not just that David counted people. The real offense was that David was COUNTING ON people. And whatever you count on is in competition with God; particularly if God already sees you as a person in deep covenant relationship with Him as David was. God has a strong tendency to start killing what you are counting- or rather, counting on. Herein laid the dilemma and catastrophe David faced. It was a terrible season in his life. Oh I pray just in case we have offended God that we do not see the other side of Him!

When a believer finds himself in a situation whereby he has fallen out of favour with God, what can he do? When the sword of judgement has been raised over your territory of influence, what should be done? When you know you have blown it and messed up irreparably before the eyes of men, what can be done to remedy the situation? When God Himself is angry at your foolishness, when God's wrath starts to chew at you, what solution can you employ?

The answers to these questions reveal one of the secrets of the keys of David. This is one of the mysteries behind the sure mercies that David enjoyed-i.e. the guaranteed mercies of David. That means if you do the same thing that David did, you are sure to experience the same intervention of mercy- GUARANTEED! (2 Samuel 24: 18)
A prophetic Word came to David from the prophet of God instructing him to raise an altar of sacrifice. Then David made a very profound statement revealing a major

secret key to averting divine judgement. (2 Samuel 24:24)

The answer is to raise an altar which cost you something with a heart of genuine repentance and along sides the cry for mercy. Do not just give something that would not cost you. Bring a costly sacrifice to the altar and the plague of divine judgement shall be averted. This is one of David's secrets. No wonder he found much more mercy than his predecessor King Saul.

If you discover that you come from a family lineage of ancestors that had earned the judgement of God via wicked acts, and now you are suffering from the sins you knew nothing about, it is time to raise an altar of true repentance with a sacrifice that costs you something, and the plague shall cease.

This is a mystery of David's altar. If it worked for David, then it will work for you also because you are also a seed of David through Jesus Christ. Praise God!

CHAPTER 3

ALTARS AND WITCHCRAFT

Witchcraft is the principal agent of the altars who execute ancestral and generational miseries.

3
ALTARS AND WITCHCRAFT

WITCHCRAFT is the major agent of satan involved in attacking and stealing from humanity their God given destines. He is involved in all wicked strategies and manipulations against humanity. He fights subtly and wisely. He devices various means to implicate humanity right from infancy. He creates problems and solutions so as to trap you.

Witchcraft is the principal agent of the altars who execute ancestral and generational miseries. Witchcraft is the greatest enemy of mankind whose aim is to deny you from producing evidence in your generation. He is the destroyer of man's marital and family destiny. He denies you the impact you should make in your world. Witchcraft manipulates people out of the way of grace into the part of disgrace.

He covers your marital, financial, academic and business star from shining and makes your potentials and talents irrelevant to your generation. Witchcraft prolongs your stay in struggle, hardship, single-hood, marital hardship, barrenness, tears and sorrows.

He is the power behind strange and prolonged sickness like the woman in Mark 5 who had the issue of blood for 12 years, the woman in Luke 13:10 who was bowed over for eighteen years and the man in John 5 at the pool of Bethesda for 38 years. When witchcraft is behind a sickness, medical science is not only helpless but irrelevant!

Witchcraft is the power behind mysterious financial hardship and indebtedness. He is the power in charge of mysterious disappointment and disfavour. Witchcraft has made potential husbands and wives to remain unmarried. He has made potential parents childless. He has turned multimillionaires into beggars. Witchcraft has collapsed many businesses with great future. Rich and influential people in our society have been brought to nothing by this spirit. Burden lifters, rescuers, answers and solution agents in families, villages and the society have died before their time by this spirit. This is a very serious issue!

Witchcraft is the power that wastes people's seasons so that they cannot produce evidence in their time.

> *So teach us to number our days, that we may apply our hearts unto wisdom. Psalms 90:12*

HOW DOES HE OPERATE?

Altars are where humanity meets invisible powers for help, covenants and dedications. It also includes certain cultural practices and occultic involvements that exalt satan. Any cultural practice that establish demonic activities into an individual, family and village, is an altar. The power of witchcraft is the EVIL ALTAR in your background. Witchcraft is the power assigned to execute the decisions of the EVIL ALTARS. What the Holy Spirit is to the church is what witchcraft is to the satanic kingdom. Just as the church is powerless without the Holy Spirit, so also the satanic kingdom is powerless without witchcraft. Where ever there is an evil altar, witchcraft is present. It is the ultimate assignment of witchcraft powers to manipulate people into doing or saying things that will enable them execute the decisions of the altar. Therefore if you must destroy witchcraft, you must first of all destroy the altars that sponsor them. Your primary enemy is the altar.

The operations of witchcraft and the Altars is like the operations of the Airport, Aircraft and the Pilot. The Airport is the Altar. The Airport is where you have the Control Tower that decides when any plane should take off' or land. The Airplane is the satanic system called Craft. The Pilot is the Witch who practices or operates the Craft. Note that the airplane and the pilot cannot function without the Airport where you have the Control Tower and the runway. In the same way, witchcraft cannot function without Altars.

Where ever you see witchcraft activities operating is an indication that there are altars that have not been destroyed. Witchcraft operates in disguise and subtlety. They will stain you with some point of contact without your knowledge and this enables them to operate in your life. Witchcraft is the manipulative power of the satanic kingdom who takes advantage of the ignorance of his victim. He engages in short and long term strategies.

ABRAHAM. GEN. 13:1-18

He manipulated Abraham to take Lot along and that hindered him from seeing all that God had for him. By virtue of this action, His destiny was delayed.

> *And Abram went up out of Egypt, he, and his wife, and all that he had, and Lot with him, into the south. Gen 13:1*

He made him go down to Egypt so as to get a house maid that will become his mistress and produce a child that will breed a generation of violet men in the world.

> *Now Sarai Abram's wife bare him no children: and she had an handmaid, an Egyptian, whose name was Hagar. And Sarai said unto Abram, Behold now, the LORD hath restrained me from bearing: I pray thee, go in unto my maid; it may be that I may obtain children by her. And Abram hearkened to the voice of Sarai. And Sarai Abram's wife took Hagar her maid the Egyptian, after Abram had dwelt ten years in the land of Canaan, and gave her to her husband Abram to be his wife. And he went in unto Hagar, and she conceived: and when she saw that she had*

conceived, her mistress was despised in her eyes.
Gen 16:1-4

MOSES. EXODUS 2:1-25

He manipulated his mother to take certain actions which gave him false identity for 40 yrs. He could not decide for himself. Just like multitude today who are victims of parental decisions and covenants. Mysterious relocation is responsible for fragmented destinies.

His destiny was delayed for 80ys. His name Moses (brought out of the water) implicated him and denied him entrance into the Promised Land.

SAMSON JUDGES 16.

Witchcraft manipulated Samson, a man anointed from the womb, inflicted him with sexual immorality, took his garment of power and glory, ended his ministry and life untimely. He hijacked his destiny.

DAVID. 2 SAMUEL 11

He attacked David a man after God's heart to commit adultery and murder so as to affect his children. David's action introduced the evil pattern of immorality and murder amongst his children which finally led to the division of the kingdom after Solomon's reign.

SOLOMON. 1 KINGS 11:1-14

Witchcraft manipulated him to marry many strange women who turned his heart away from the Lord who broke protocol and made him a king instead of his elder brother. He raised strange altars for his wives and brought Gods anger on his family .This affected his children's inheritance. His first son lost a greater part of the kingdom to a servant.

ESAU GEN. 25:29-34

He manipulated him to sell his future, his birthright, for a present satisfaction, a plate of porridge. He gave him present satisfaction with complicated future troubles.

GEHAZI. 2 KINGS 5

He manipulated him to collect what his master the prophet rejected. He wanted to arrive before time. He took a short cut that cut his life short. He got leprosy instead of the double portion of the anointing. He set up the evil pattern of leprosy for his children and the unborn generation.

Witchcraft manipulated our fathers to raise evil altars that have implicated their children's destinies. Our fathers raised altars to meet their needs and deny us our needs. This is the real reason why we must fight to ensure that we are totally delivered from the mistakes of our fathers and their consequences.

> *Remember, O LORD, what is come upon us: consider, and behold our reproach. Our inheritance is turned to strangers, our houses to aliens. We are orphans and fatherless, our mothers are as widows. We have drunken our water for money; our wood is sold unto us. Our necks are under persecution: we labour, and have no rest. We have given the hand to the Egyptians, and to the Assyrians, to be satisfied with bread. Our fathers have sinned, and are not; and we have borne their iniquities. Servants have ruled over us: there is none that doth deliver us out of their hand.*
> *Lam 5:1-8*

STRANGE HAPPENINGS TODAY *LAM. 5:1-17*

There are virtually no families in the spectrum of Africa without a traceable link to one altar or another. Whether the altar is active or seemingly dormant, the fact is an altar is in existence or once existed. In my over three decades in ministry, I have seen very disturbing things happen to people as a result of the operations of altars raised in the past, that are still speaking against the descendants of those who raised the altars.

Long after our great-grandparents, ancestors and patriarchs/matriarchs of our families have died; the altars they believed in are still speaking loud with strange patterns and cycles that leave their victims confused.

My many years of struggling both in ministry and family life had its basis on the fact that altars of my family lineage were contending against me and I had no knowledge. I had no prior information that there were unknown "contracts" or covenant from my own family line that forbade a proper wedding and marriage; I was breaking the law of that evil covenant that spoke from the family altar. Nobody told me early enough.

Many precious saints are labouring under the heavy weight of burdens they had unknowingly inherited from the altars of their fathers. The mere fact that you are in Christ with a commitment to worship God, instead of the gods of the altars of your biological bloodline, puts you in a position of endless contention, until you take a real stand after being armed with the knowledge of this serious matter.

For example, many pastors and preachers may never succeed in the work of their ministries because, many years ago their great-grandfathers who themselves were priests to other gods and deities, had already dedicated their lineage to the service of those altars. So, a decision to obey the call to the ministry would be seen as an affront or an insult. These pastors are breaking the agreement. It is time for the deliverer to deliver himself. If pastors are not exempted, what makes you think that the average Christian is free to live life like an endless holiday season?

One of my daughters in faith fell dangerously sick on her wedding day. She was carried from her wedding reception to be admitted in the hospital, in her wedding gown! She knew she was to die if she did not act fast so she asked to call me to pray for her. After the prayer, she was discharged the next day! Many young people do not know that their marital testimony have been traded on strange altars in the past, forbidding that they ever get married. It is time to grow up and take spiritual responsibility.

Young man and woman, the enemy is taking your matter seriously. There is therefore no reason why you should not then take your matter even more seriously than the enemy himself!

An ambitious man coming from a lineage of strugglers and failures, managed to attempt traveling out of the country. When he arrived at the airport of the foreign country, he discovered that his intentional passport was nowhere to be found. He searched desperately but to no avail. Eventually, he was deported to his home country. He was very devastated. On returning to his village, he met his elderly uncle at home. After welcoming him back home, that uncle simply entered the bedroom, opened his old cupboard, brought out the young man's passport and gave it to him back. "You are a small boy", he told the young man, with a mocking tone. Please understand that life is a battleground of altars. That old man may have been the custodian of the family's altars, supervising the slavery of all the family members. Beloved, it is time to pray aggressively to the point of total deliverance.

Ask yourself these questions; who is fighting me? Who did this to me? Who is manipulating an evil altar against my desired testimony?

Anything you do not want, you do not watch!

A couple had been trying to have a child for over fifteen years. During their deliverance prayers, it was revealed that the woman's family had demanded for a virgin she-goat among other dowry requirements during the traditional wedding. Needless to say, something was done with the virgin goat on an evil altar, thereby hindering the wife's ability to ever conceive. It is time to question certain traditional requests or demands and apply God's wisdom on these matters.

Some families are suffering under the weight of harrowing poverty because the deities of their villages forbid financial prosperity. No business venture would ever become profitable. No family member has ever owned a car, university degree or any other form of meaningful achievement. Yet, nobody in such families is asking vital questions. Why are we all experiencing individual and collective poverty in this family? Why are we all having area boys, hoodlums, vagabonds, prostitutes, etc. in this family? What is happening?

A certain graduate who has been in search of a job for a while was invited for a job interview with a good company. During the interview, he seemed to be answering the questions of his interviewer with correct responses. Obviously, he was bright, intelligent and very promising. Just as he was about to gain favour on the job interview, something mysterious occurred; a big cockroach quietly crawled out of his shirt pocket in full view of the interviewer! Then, a second and third cockroach crawled out. You know the end of the story. He lost favour immediately. The interviewer became disgusted.

Children of God, cry out bitterly in prayers, invoking the vengeance of God against any altar supervising you at the point of your breakthroughs.

Let me make this very clear. Do not say these things cannot be at operation in your own family. You would be amazed at how covenants made on your behalf long before you were born are quietly waiting for your season of highest happiness and greatest vulnerability. Take nothing for granted.

There are no little altars, there are only belittled ones.

How would you explain the case of a woman who had waited for a baby for some years, decided to walk away from the Church of Jesus to ask go ask a fetish priest for a baby? Yes, she eventually got a male child after 9 months. She even defended herself before others that God was too slow for her. So, she had to find a way to "help God". The important thing was to just have a child or so she thought. Seven years later, the little boy entered her bedroom, demanding that his mother take off her clothes for him. In shock, she demanded to know why. The little boy replied, "because I want to have sex!" The fetish altar that had given her that child had started speaking in both her life and the life of that child.

What altars have you or your parents/ancestors ever been involved with and are still claiming ownership of a department of your life? It is time to denounce and deliver yourself and your family from these influences.

A lady had been waiting for a life partner for many years. After a time of joint deliverance prayers, a revelation came asking for who had given her the first bath immediately after her birth? It was revealed that an old woman in the village did so. She was told to go and demand for the very sponge that was used on her. She went to the old woman and found her in the village. This old woman took her into her fetish altar room. The young lady saw many sponges; all still soaked. That wicked woman still recognized that particular young lady's sponge and returned it to her still dripping with water after nearly thirty five years. When she returned to the deliverance session, the sponge was burnt and she was set free. Not long after, her long awaited husband found her. Unknown to her, an altar had been raised at her birth that contended with her future marriage. Don't ever belittle your trials particularly when you are noticing a questionable family pattern. Give full attention to details that seem strange. Turn that unending matter that is causing you shame into a reason to engage in aggressive battle in prayers. It is your time to silence both the altars and those who raise them against you. Precious child of God, this is your finest hour. It is time to lift up your voice to the rooftop of prayers and declare war for your sake and the sake of your children and future generation.

ARISE, CRY OUT IN THE NIGHT: in the beginning of the watches pour out thine heart like water before the face of the Lord: lift up thy hands toward him for the life of thy young children, that faint for hunger in the top of every street. Lam 2:19

According to Archbishop Benson Idahosa, "If there is a man to pray, there is a God to answer". He will never reject the sincere cry of His children. Go ahead and cry!!!

CHAPTER 4

OPERATIONS
OF THE ALTARS

Without the backing of God's altar, your life can be altered on satanic altars.

4

OPERATIONS
OF THE ALTARS

Whatever you see as the operations of the negative altar is a counterfeit of what is obtainable on the Altar of God. In the Bible times of old, the Altar was the bearer of the presence of God amongst the people. The Israelites understood that each territory they found themselves in already had altars dedicated to strange gods and evil deities. They therefore entered each new area with the raising of an Altar dedicated to the God of Israel, the Lord Jehovah whom they served. They would not enter any unfamiliar territory lightly and carelessly.

This explains why in all of Father Abraham's journey, at each major entering of any new land, he would raise an Altar to God with a sacrifice on that Altar. *(Genesis 12:1-2, 6-7, 8-9, 13:3-4, 18)*

> *Now the LORD had said unto Abram, Get thee out of thy country, and from thy kindred, and from thy father's house, unto a land that I will shew thee: And I will make of thee a great nation, and I will bless thee, and make thy name great; and thou shalt be a blessing: And I will bless them that bless thee,*

and curse him that curseth thee: and in thee shall all families of the earth be blessed. Genesis 12:1-3)And Abram passed through the land unto the place of Sichem, unto the plain of Moreh. And the Canaanite was then in the land. And the LORD appeared unto Abram, and said, Unto thy seed will I give this land: and there builded he an ALTAR unto the LORD, who appeared unto him. And he removed from thence unto a mountain on the east of Bethel, and pitched his tent, having Bethel on the west, and Hai on the east: and there he builded an ALTAR unto the LORD, and called upon the name of the LORD. Gen 12:6-8

THE ALTAR HELPS YOU TO POSSESS YOUR POSSESION

In Genesis 12:6-7, God gave Abraham the land of the Canaanites. In verse 6 he saw that the Canaanites were in the land, which means a principality was in charge of the land. Abraham knew that what has been given to him has been in the hand of some strange altars hence he raised his own altar to contend with them. DEUT. 2:24. What you are interested in, someone else is interested in it. The man or woman you want to marry some other persons are interested in them. The position you desire is also desired by someone else and it is a case of the highest bidder. The highest bidder wins in life. You can't fold your hand and watch what you want be taken by your fellow contenders. Those contending with you have altars they constantly service and you must service your altar to win your opponent.

You win life battles by the voice of your altars. Sacrifice is the voice of the altar, that's the reason why people sacrifice constantly on the altar. The more you sacrifice, the more strong voice you provoke.

The evil nail fastened on your issue is fastened on the altar by sacrifice and it will take your sacrifice to provoke heaven to remove the nail.

In that day, saith the LORD of hosts, shall the nail that is fastened in the sure place be removed, and be cut down, and fall; and the burden that was upon it shall be cut off: for the LORD hath spoken it. (Isaiah 22:25)

The reason men bury live cows and shed blood on their altars is to empower witchcraft to help them, manipulate, overpower and win their opponents. You are stagnant and loosing the battles because you have not raised a stronger altar against the enemy of your destiny.

The secret to win this long standing battle is in your hand .Your opponent's strongest weapon is the voice of his sacrifice on the altar. Arise and overcome them by raising your own altar .

Only desperate and wise contenders win in the affairs of life nobody can win for you. You have to do it. It may be painful but that is what it takes to win.

Make that sacrifice now. Challenge your contenders by

provoking God's altar to fight for you.

A drunkard went to diviner to find out why his life was in a total mess. The diviner brought out two empty calabashes and put black cloth in the one on the right and white clothe on the one on the left. He took a wall gecko and told the man that if the wall gecko enters the calabash with white clothe then his destiny will be great but if it enters the black one then his destiny is ruined. As he watch the wall gecko move to the calabash with black clothe he took the wall gecko by force and put it in the calabash with white clothe. The diviner got angry and asked him why he did what he did, the drunkard said "I can't watch my life ruined in my presence". I have to act fast before it is late.

Friend you must not watch your life ruined while you have the chance to make a change. Whoever is standing on your case is backed by the power of strange altars and you must also engage the altar of God to stop them before they finish you.

Even Jacob when fleeing from the death threat of his brother Esau whom he had cheated of his birth right stumbled upon an Altar location around a vicinity called Bethel. This Bethel was one of the many places Abraham had once raised an Altar about two generations prior. Yet, the Altar was still active because, angels were still ascending and descending a stair case ladder, attending to that spot where he slept for the night.

And Jacob went out from Beer-sheba, and went

toward Haran. And he lighted upon a certain place, and tarried there all night, because the sun was set; and he took of the stones of that place, and put them for his pillows, and lay down in that place to sleep. And he dreamed, and behold a ladder set up on the earth, and the top of it reached to heaven: and behold the angels of God ascending and descending on it. And, behold, the LORD stood above it, and said, I am the LORD God of Abraham thy father, and the God of Isaac: the land whereon thou liest, to thee will I give it, and to thy seed; And thy seed shall be as the dust of the earth, and thou shalt spread abroad to the west, and to the east, and to the north, and to the south: and in thee and in thy seed shall all the families of the earth be blessed. And, behold, I am with thee, and will keep thee in all places whither thou goest, and will bring thee again into this land; for I will not leave thee, until I have done that which I have spoken to thee of. And Jacob awaked out of his sleep, and he said, Surely the LORD is in this place; and I knew it not. And he was afraid, and said, How dreadful is this place! this is none other but the house of God, and this is the gate of heaven. And Jacob rose up early in the morning, and took the stone that he had put for his pillows, and set it up for a pillar, and poured oil upon the top of it. And he called the name of that place Bethel: but the name of that city was called Luz at the first. And Jacob vowed a vow, saying, If God will be with me, and will keep me in this way that I go, and will give me bread to eat, and raiment to put on, So that I come again to my

father's house in peace; then shall the LORD be my
God: And this stone, which I have set for a pillar,
shall be God's house: and of all that thou shalt give
me I will surely give the tenth unto thee.
Genesis 28:10-22

In the days of Moses, the Lord instructed him to build the Ark of Covenant. This was an Altar, carrying God's presence in the Old Testament dispensation which can be referred to as a mobile Altar.

When the Ark was brought to the battlefield, Israel won the battles. Even when it seemed like the Ark had been captured by the enemy and brought into the altar room or shrine of dagon, the god of the philistines, the Ark which is the Altar of God brought their idol to prostrate *1 Samuel 5:1-7* and eventually cut it to pieces.

God's Altar does not need your help. It is already empowered. It is already potent. The Ark Altar killed Uzza who tried to help it. The same Ark Altar was welcomed into the house of Obededom and he became a wealthy man *2 Samuel 6:10 -12*. The Altar of God when valued properly prospers you any day, anytime.

If you will pay close attention to the things God is saying to you in this book, you would be amazed at the amazing results you would be able to generate from the knowledge and depth of insight available herein.

Contrary to the false teachings in certain quarters today, the New Testament (or New Covenant), did not change the mystery or dynamic operations of the Altar. The mysteries of the altars still apply. The only difference is that the sacrifice has changed. Jesus Christ is the acceptable sacrifice on the Altar. He is the Lamb that was slain or sacrificed from the foundation of the world. Meaning, before the world began, God has already raised an Altar that would speak for us. God has already beaten our enemies to the altar game. Our enemies came too late.

> *And all that dwell upon the earth shall worship him, whose names are not written in the book of life of the Lamb slain from the foundation of the world. Rev 13:8*

Understanding the mystery of the altar and its operations will help you gain sure victories in the battles of life.

There is power behind the Altar – whether negative or positive.

A young man full of zeal went to the altar shrine of his family and maybe because he was a baby Christian; in a bid to disregard and mock the altar, he decided to deliberately urinate on the shrine. Unfortunately, that was the last time his "manhood" worked just from mocking altar forces that were older than his father and were probably ruling over his bloodline.

Do you realize that certain trees in your villages are probably altars? A young lady at the age of sixteen was in a sexual relationship with a man. When she decided to end the relationship maybe for another person, she was beaten seriously. With bitterness in her heart, she went out at midnight, stood under a banana tree and placed a curse on the man. She did that while holding onto her breasts and private part; she was stark naked. Unfortunately, she probably thought she was alone as she stood under that tree.

Six months later, the young man whom she cursed was afflicted with a strange illness and died. Maybe she got what she wanted, but decades later, at around fifty, she is yet to find a husband till date. The pertinent questions are as follows; was she alone under the banana tree as she released bitter venom in speech against the man who beat her? Were there other 'witnesses' having their personal conferences at the tree around their altar? Who taught a sixteen year old girl how to go spiritual in the negative sense, to avenge another?

I pity foolish young men who are playing away their season. The evil witnessed at that time of the night under that tree empowered her words by giving her what she wanted, but then also exchanged her martial destiny for what she never wanted. She is still single and searching and already, age is no longer on her side.

Are you aware that sometimes, a person can himself become an altar? This is dependent on how deeply entrenched the person is. A human being can be turned to an altar. Some great men of God today have walked with God very deeply for years that their very lives is a mobile Altar for God. Anything you place in their hands as a quality seed or gift will surely multiply in your favour. This happened in the case of Elijah, the Prophet and the widow of Zarephath. This also happened when they gave Jesus five loaves and two fishes.

In the negative realm, certain persons have so soaked themselves in evil covenant with satanic altars such that their lives are Satan's mobile shrines.

Many people in diverse professions such as business, politics, entertainment, media and many other spheres have sold their souls to the devil. Be careful who you partner with.

Your daughter in the university comes home with a brand new car from a 'boyfriend' the age of your forefathers and you seem not to be bothered?

A young lady told me of a scenario in which an older man; a politician, came to their campus hostel and invited her and her friends to his hotel room. What is a man in his sixties doing with girls his daughters' age? If not that he is on a mission to service his altars?

In his hotel room that night (after trying to drug them to sleep), her friend slept off under the influence of the drink, but she pretended to be asleep. The elderly man brought out a snake from a magical box after certain incantations and put it in her friend's body through her private area and brought it out again. By morning, he dismissed them with a payment of Hundreds of

Thousands of Naira each.

On arrival to her hostel, the said girl went into the shower to have her bath. As she turned on the shower for water, blood began to flow through her private part. She slumped and died on the spot! Somebody had used her soul to service his altar as a sacrifice. It was an unfortunate situation.

The world we live in is not a playground, rather it is a battleground. Its time we reconnect to the mysteries of our own Altar in Christ Jesus to quench every evil contention sent from negative altars.

AFRICAN ALTARS

There are altars controlling individuals, marriages, families, villages, cities, nations, and even whole continents. It is not news that the very continent of Africa is deeply entrenched in the curses and covenants of altars that had held sway for several generations.

African slaves exported witchcraft, magic and idolatry to other regions of the world; for example, to the Caribbean (Haiti, Trinidad and Tobago amongst others) and South America (Brazil). The influence of generational family altar may be the reason why Africans in diaspora continue to be known for violence, theft crime, gang wars, etc. Why is that? A small Agama lizard on African soil will not become an alligator in America. The altar forces in the black man's bloodline may still be speaking. Only by taking cover in the Blood of the Lamb can he fully maximize his true destiny.

The altars in the African Countries are very active. Certain tribes in Africa served war gods in their past generations. How then can these regions have peace among their ethnic groups? The altar of their gods will call for blood every fifty years or less according to the covenant they enacted centuries ago. Until the Blood of the Prince of Peace washes over these territories and villages via fervent prayers, all attempts at diplomatic peace treaties will continue to be rubbished by these wicked spirit of tribal wars. The Church of Jesus in those regions must rise up and take their stand.

Which altar was raised during the independence of the African nations? Which "heroes" of emancipation raised them on behalf of their nation, which the masses celebrated in ignorance? Every Independence Day is supposed to be a time of unanimously raising of the Altar of Jesus upon the land crying for God's mercy over the land and covering the people with the Blood of The Lamb.

Yes, it is that serious! It is Altar versus altar- even on a national scale.

Altars have spirits. Altars have procedures. So, whatever time you have an opportunity to bring a sacrifice to the Altar in church, take that act very seriously. Realize that certain forces are present- the angelic spirits and the Spirit of God over the commission of the altar of that ministry.

Know also that for any altar to exist there must have been a priest involved. In the kingdom of God as well as in the satanic world, priesthood is an indispensable part of altar operations.

CHAPTER

5

STRANGE SIGNS
OF WICKED ALTARS
AT WORK

You cannot intelligently confront what you don't understand

5

STRANGE SIGNS
OF WICKED
ALTARS AT WORK

Altars are one of the most powerful secrets of this world. At the hands of the wicked altars become instruments of evil and deadly weapons of mass destruction. An altar in God's kingdom can become a place of divine power and a promotion centre where destinies find God's raw grace to excel and prosper.

Over the ages, countless generations have been victims of evil altars. These altars have been responsible for many unfortunate incidents that have left many confused and helpless. The operations of these evil altars raised by the wicked have rendered some once promising future stars end up as candles whose light have been blown out by the wind. Many who should be celebrating today are living in perpetual sorrow.

As one of God's appointed generals in the school of deliverance and warfare, I think I can say with the preacher in *Ecclesiastes 10-* , that I have seen rulers- born kings- walk on foot while slaves ride on the horses belonging to those kings. Foolish people have been treated as worthy while the wise have been treated as unworthy. Why? Some force is holding sway, all on the platform of an altar either visible or invisible.

There is an evil which I have seen under the sun, as an error which proceedeth from the ruler: Folly is set in great dignity, and the rich sit in low place. I have seen servants upon horses, and princes walking as servants upon the earth. Eccl 10:5-7

There are several noticeable signs that show that an altar is currently at work. Certain strange occurrences when constantly repeated could be a clear signal to the discerning person that something beyond the ordinary is going on. When there is pain, the foolish become scattered and loses balance while the wise gathers his thoughts, observe and embarks on a serious research process. The wise knows that Nothing Just Happens. I want you to be that wise one.

The following are some noticeable strange signs that act as pointers to the presence of the activities of evil altars at work in a person's life, family or a given place or territory. **Strange Unending Poverty Cycles**: You may notice this in many households. Everybody is poor in that family. The father, mother, brother, sister, aunty, uncle, children and grandparents. As a matter of fact, it is normal to find them poor; so poor that even the poor in town call them poor. Such families never have a voice in the society. The Bible says the voice of the poor man is never heard, no matter how wise he may claim to be.

Now there was found in it a poor wise man, and he

> *by his wisdom delivered the city; yet no man remembered that same poor man. Then said I, Wisdom is better than strength: nevertheless the poor man's wisdom is despised, and his words are not heard. Eccl 9:15-16*

They are the poorest of the poor. In such families, the normal thing for every child would be to grow up and become a housemaid somewhere either in exchange for inferior education or feeding.

Jesus knew how dangerous this plague of poverty was which was why He made it the first of His projects in the preaching of the Gospel.

> *The Spirit of the Lord is upon me, because he hath anointed me to PREACH THE GOSPEL TO THE POOR; he hath sent me to heal the brokenhearted, to preach deliverance to the captives, and recovering of sight to the blind, to set at liberty them that are bruised. Luke 4:18*

When a family experiences bombardment of transgenerational poverty, they live their lives without rewards. This strange cycle moves from just the lack of physical cash into realms of their minds; i.e. poverty mentality plagues them all. Such a person, family and nation under this yoke of altar of poverty will never dare to attempt big things in life.

And of course, no man can ever become great in life until he dares to bite more than he can chew at some point in life. So these people are born poor, live poor, school poor, marry poor, have poor parents, choose poor friends, plan poor, age poor and poorly, die poor and are buried poor- leaving behind no inheritance or investments for children but debts, unending sorrow and a haunting memory of poverty experience for the generations unborn because the altars of poverty have ravaged their lives and families.

You must get angry against the altar of poverty and turn this strange occurrence into a project. Some families cannot even see that it is a matter of urgency. That in itself is the blinding spirit of the altar of poverty at work. It is time to be free!

Strange Cycles of Sickness

Certain families take this matter lightly. You would notice that certain homes are experiencing predictable cycle of sickness or certain sicknesses. In fact, at some point, you hear them referring to it in this manner saying, "Our sickness". How pathetic!

In some families, you see a strange cycle of blood diseases, in others; cases of reproductive sicknesses, several forms of cancer that moves from one generation to another. When you notice that what killed your grandparents have now killed your parents, my dear friend, it is not the time to go to sleep or cry and cower in fear of "whose next"? It is a wakeup call as you have walked into the knowledge of the fact that there is an altar operating somewhere. Tell yourself "the altar responsible for this continuous pattern of family illness will not speak in my own life". An observant Christian is empowered with the ability to win ALL the battles of life. Please take note of strange cycles of diseases constantly plaguing the family tree or bloodline. An evil altar is active somewhere.

Strange Cases of Sin and Moral or Character Failure

Such patterns may have been noticed in a family lineage. Certain sins stand out in certain families. In some households, every grown up is an adulterer. It is normal so they think. Drunkenness is the family bane in some places. Others, it is incest- siblings sleeping with each other.

Some people are trans-generational thieves. Grandfather was a thief, father a thief, so what is expected of the children of that family?

A strange altar of sin is speaking. You must not watch it. Fight it!

Whatever mystery of iniquity is chewing you and your family raw should be sought out; an altar may be active in that area.

Strange Cycles of Failure

In certain families, no one ever seems to achieve their goals in life. No ambition works. They only experience the unfortunate "near success" syndrome. A few minutes away from success and without any tangible explanation or cogent reason especially to the physical eyes, it passes away. No matter how sincere or well-intended they maybe or appear to be, they just do not achieve nor attain. Everybody else gets "there" but not them. Phrases such as "could have, would have and should have" are always found present in the details when they are sharing the stories of their lives.

They may pursue, but they always miss the target. If you see such happening in an unending predictable pattern or cycle, then realise that a strange altar is busy speaking out loud and clear! The altar of failure.

Strange Cycles of Marital Problems

This is a notable trait in many families where it is normal to have failed marriages or no marriages at all. They encounter several wrong marital relationships. Polygamy reigns supreme. Some are presented with situations where it is normal to find parents, uncles, aunties who have married at least thrice, with the partners all still alive. Something which cannot be explained keeps fighting the existence of any serious marriage. Wedding ceremonies, if any, are just mere formalities. The regular outcome of such marriages is known to all and the resultant effect expected within a given period of time. Needless to say, a strange altar is speaking against the union. This should not be trivialized.

In another angle, some families discover that people do not get married the right way. For others, it is late marriage, and another, their young men and women of marriageable age do not find marriage partners and are faced with a lot of negative pressure from their parents and sometimes nosey family members. They are sometimes faced with a situation where their parents push them out with hurtful statements like, "I am tired of waiting for you to get your acts together! Just go out there and get me grandchildren before I die!". It is a very pathetic situation and circumstance to find oneself in.

It is also very strange but it is happening and many are held in the bondage of the existence of such occurrences. End of the year festive seasons e.g. Christmas can become sorrowful times for the singles as they are made to bear being taunted and harassed with mockery. "So, the year has come and gone again, just the same as last year and you have returned home as usual without a man or (woman). Well, if you do not deem it fit to get married, please just ensure you get me a grandchild anyhow even if it means getting it from an already married person!" These are signs of an active strange altars speaking against the fulfillment of the marital destinies of such affected families.

Strange Cycles of Childlessness and Barrenness

It is pertinent that one is observant enough to catch such repeated occurrence functional at different times to different relatives all in one family. It is a case of an evil declaration from a wicked altar. In some families, certain couples from a certain family tree are denied one gender at childbirth. In some cases, they are denied children of the male gender and in others, children of the other sex. . Please note that not all families that have a particular sex of children born to them are facing negative family altars but for some according to a repeated pattern or cycle and after aggressive prayers and revelation may come to the knowledge and light of the exact situation they may be facing.. Infertility may be a sign of an active altar at work, particularly where the cases are rampant in one family.

......the lists of these strange signs vary and are numerous. You just have to be sensitive and very observant to watch out for strange and questionable negative patterns and occurrences that keep rising up every now and then in the family. These can act as pointers to the presence of evil altar speaking.

Mysterious Cycles of Death: Some families have found themselves in very mysterious episodes of the deaths of men.

Evil altars sponsor witchcraft activities in people's lives which is usually responsible for mysterious financial, marital and business crises.

God's altar promotes angelic assignment for miraculous financial, marriage, business, academic and professional breakthroughs.

Evil altars draw the line of limitations and delays in family. Luke 10:30.

God's altar breaks limitations and sponsors speed in the affairs of your life.

Evil altars sponsor evil patterns in family such as

divorce, late marriages, untimely death, polygamy, Death before 30, Blindness of men at 25, women whose husband died at a particular age, families with wealthy women yet no husbands and families with married men who are all ravaged by poverty.

God's altar sponsors positive patters of longevity in life, stability and good marriages, consistent progress and prosperity.

Evil altars sponsor generational courses and issues and collective poverty.

God's altars sponsor generational blessings and progress. Abraham.

Evil altars sponsor repetitions of negative family history. God's altars sponsor repetitions of positive family history.

Evil altars sponsor manifestation of evil covenants and dedications.

God's altars sponsor manifestations of good covenants. Evil altars are prison house where destinies of members are held captives.

God's altars provoke release of destinies of family members.

Evil altars make you a lawful captives (Isaiah 49:24)

God's altars are where promises and covenants of freedoms and liberties are made.

Altars sponsors ancestral penalties.

THE VICTORY OF THE ALTAR OF CALVARY

"Lo this, we have searched it, so it is, hear it, and know thou it is for thy good" Job 5:27

The lessons you have opportunity to learn in these pages are for your own good. They are not to make you afraid, neither is this book written to make you feel helpless about a bad situation. That is not the purpose this book is aimed at, rather, this book is bearing tidings of Good News, to tell you that there is a way out of that tough predicament you may have found yourself. God is determined to make your case different as long as you are a child of God and you have accepted Jesus Christ as your personal Lord and Saviour.

Jesus Christ, on the Cross of Calvary conquered the principalities and powers of this wicked world, making an open show of them in everlasting triumph. These principalities and powers are the forces behind the activities of the wicked altars speaking against you and your family.

Blotting out the handwriting of ordinances that was against us, which was contrary to us, and took it out of the way, nailing it to his cross; And having spoiled

*principalities and powers, he made a shew of them
openly, triumphing over them in it. Col 2:14-15*

"God in His great love for you delivered you from the
power of darkness and translated us into the kingdom
where His Son Jesus rules supreme as King".

> *Giving thanks unto the Father, which hath made
> us meet to be partakers of the inheritance of the
> saints in light: Who hath delivered us from the
> power of darkness, and hath translated us into the
> kingdom of his dear Son. Col 1:12-13*

A closer study of the New Testament documents clearly
reveal that God sent Jesus to give us both victory over
evil altars and their strange patterns in our lives and that
the death, resurrection and ascension of Jesus Christ
repositioned us to sit together with King Jesus in
heavenly places. This superior positioning empowers us
to operate from the highest cadre of ruler ship and
spiritual warfare- FAR ABOVE PRINCIPALITIES
AND POWERS (the defeated forces behind mysterious
evil altars). Jesus gave us victory when He gave the
triumphant cry, "IT IS FINISHED!" Meaning "IT IS
ACCOMPLISHED!"

He accomplished absolute conquest for us once and for
all. By the sacrifice of His Blood and the Word of His
testimony on the Cross- "It is finished!"

Thus, we have overcome by the Blood of the Lamb and
by the Words of our testimony.

Now it behoves on us as His own priests to deploy that very Blood shed on Calvary's Altar as we speak Words of testimony; testifying, enforcing and agreeing that Jesus has given us victory over the wicked altar forces threatening our inheritances in God. This is the Battle we are engaged in. We are not "trying" to win. We are fighting to take into possession our victory "having already been declared winners" for He has made us "more than conquerors".

> *Nay, in all these things we are more than conquerors through him that loved us. Rom 8:37*

Jesus is the Ultimate High Priest in the battle of altars. There can be no altar without a priest. Our Altar in the kingdom of God is the highest and the most supreme….we have a High Priest of our profession of victory through faith in the Blood of Jesus.

> *Wherefore, holy brethren, partakers of the heavenly calling, consider the Apostle and High Priest of our profession, Christ Jesus. Heb 3:1*

Therefore, we cannot lose a battle because the High Priest of our Altar in heaven liveth and abideth FOREVER.

> *The LORD hath sworn, and will not repent, Thou art a priest for ever after the order of Melchizedek. Ps 110:4*

> *Whither the forerunner is for us entered, even Jesus,*

made an high priest for ever after the order of Melchisedec. Heb 6:20

The priest of all wicked altars is a dead man or a dying man. Our own High Priest is the King of life. He lives forever! Hallelujah!

KNOWING THE PROCEDURES OF THE ALTAR OF GOD

Every altar has its procedures. You cannot approach an altar without understanding the procedures that make it produce its highest benefits. How do we then lay hold on the procedures of the Altar of God's kingdom? The answer is the Word of God.

The Word of God, the Bible, is God's Book of Procedures for how God's Altar works for us, beginning from how He set the Altar of our Redemption through Christ's finished work at Calvary, and how we ought to place demands on God's power for us on the Altar in the Heavenly Holiest place, and also how we engage the Altar at the churches we belong to ensure total victory. It also reveals to us how we conduct our lives as God's Holy Temples here on earth. As mobile temples of God, we ourselves are carriers of God's mobile altars, for there can be no temple if no altar resides in it.

1 Corinthians 6: 19-20

You must therefore commit yourself to being a lifetime student of God's Word; to know and understand your rights and privileges in Christ as revealed by God's Word to us. Knowledge is the key to the deliverance of the righteous.

> *An hypocrite with his mouth destroyeth his neighbour: but through knowledge shall the just be delivered. Prov 11:9*

Take Bible studying more seriously. Read books on victorious spiritual warfare from God's anointed servants, written by those whom God has raised for the ministry of liberation, of which I am one of such vessels in our time. I say it with all humility.

Also, make yourself available for timely anointed counseling and deliverance sessions, such as we have at the Voice of Freedom Ministries- the place where God has raised an unparalleled Altar of deliverance for the emancipation of individuals, families and nations. We have seen God do it again and again. Our God never ceases to amaze me!

Testimonies:

GOD'S FAVOUR SHOWED UP FOR ME

In March 2012, I came to Benin-city homeless, stranded and confused about life because of numerous problems in my life and family. I had planned to stay with an old time girlfriend in town but I was informed that she had traveled overseas long ago. One day along the road, I came across a poster advertising a deliverance program in this church, VFM. I knew that all was not well with my life and I was unhappy so I resolved to attend and participate in the program fully. I went through the Faith Clinic teachings, the deliverance prayers and the prescribed follow up sessions. God proved Himself in my situation; and I began to experience new things in my life. Suddenly, my brother in the U.S remembered me and decided to assist me financially. I was able to start a business which is growing gradually, after a while I secured an accommodation with the help of the same brother. As if that was not enough, I was surprised when he called me one day to say that he was in Nigeria and he bought me a brand new Toyota Camry! I give all praise to God. I believe in deliverance! **Sis J. E. J.**

ANCIENT CURSES BROKEN
I began attending this Faith Clinic due to unpleasant experiences in my dreams. After one of the prayer sessions I had a dream and there was something like a seed on top of my private part which I recognized as the seed of barrenness. I succeeded in pushing it out of me. In another dream some men had been pursuing me but I turned back and started to pursue them and I killed three of them. During one of the prayer sessions, the man of God addressed the issue of curses in my life and asked me to come with sand so he can pray with me which I did. That same night in my dream three people confessed that they had used sand against me thus confirming what the man of God prayed about. One of the days as I prayed with the deliverance book (Effective Deliverance Prayers) at home I saw myself manifesting; I vomited so much. After all these ministrations the yoke is broken and I am now perfectly fine to the glory of God. **Sis. Faith E. O.**

MULTIPLE STUBBORN ATTACKS QUELLED.
I came here during the program "Freedom 2017". The last Friday of the program was the first day I attended and I came to the program totally discouraged, hopeless and depressed. True, I had a Word of assurance from God to the effect that all would be

well but I no longer believed. My entire life was a mess, I did not know what to do or where to go anymore; I had lost all hope in life and in God too. I figured that it would be a relief if my life ended then so I was not really expectant; I just wanted God to take my life. I had been a Christian for a number of years but then I backslid. In 2007 however, I came to my senses and rededicated my life to Christ- that was when all hell broke loose and my ordeal started. It was on a Sunday after I came back from church, I was sleeping in the afternoon when I had a bad dream. I saw a cousin of mine with a python and she told me that the snake liked me; but I was scared and uncomfortable with it. Before I knew what was happening, the snake gave me a bite on my back and to my surprise, when I woke up, I felt the sting on my back and that was the beginning of my woes. I was in church one day when I started seeing people that looked like British police coming to attack me with spears, as I continued to pray, things like ants were poured into my private part where they kept moving. I was living in great fear, having bad dreams and eating in the dream. As the attack continued, I started seeing python Leonora coming to attack me (hitting me, moving all over my body, lying on my back, moving round my waist etc). As these attacks were going on, I was moving from place to place, church to church looking for help and deliverance but none was forthcoming instead I grew worse. I began to feel heat sensations under my abdomen, I was seeing hoes and sticks being inserted into my private part, at a time they brought a bucket filled with tiny snakes and poured into my womb. Strange things would be crawling all over and biting me on my feet, meanwhile, the venom deposited by the serpent on my back kept reacting, giving me the feeling that I was about to suffer a cardiac arrest. I kept vomiting bitter things and some extremely sour, foamy substances. At a point, a serpent would twine itself on my left feet and my left hand attacking and hurting me.

Objects kept moving inside my stomach, and if I dared conceive, I would be in torment throughout, I would feel hands holding my two legs and pulling them apart as if attempting to tear me into two, then wooden objects would be inserted into my private part to terminate the pregnancy. One time, an invisible hand hit me on my private part between my legs and I suffered a miscarriage.
In an attempt to get my life back, I visited many places, different churches including white garments, mallams (Islamic) witch doctors, but there was no stopping the attacks instead, it kept getting worse.

I started having constant dreams of myself in my village secondary school, no one could tell me what it meant and that was how my finances kept crashing. I moved down from a woman who was having a good life and driven more than 10 cars to the point where I had none. I relocated from Kaduna to join my husband but after the relocation, I found it hard to secure a good job and when I did get one, I never received a complete salary till I left the job at the end of March 2017.

In November 2016, in my dreams, bees and scorpions started stinging me all over my anus, private part and my womb. When I lie down, they come to attack my chest and womb, when I sit; I feel something lifting me, pouring things likes needles/ arrows that hurt like fire into my womb, and private part. Sometime last year, I had a fire burn attack that affected my private part and my laps and left me with terrible itches that cause injuries, and then I developed inflammatory rashes under my breast. It was in this state that I came to Voice of Freedom Ministries. I have gone through the Faith Clinic and I stand to testify that I can now see hope where I had been so hopeless and there is light where darkness held sway. God has intervened in the attacks, and I am now pregnant and in peace. I thank God because of His great deliverance and because the devil has lost the battle over my life in Jesus' name. Amen. **Mrs. E. L. F.**

STOMACH AFFLICTION TERMINATED

For several years, I was afflicted with stomach pain; my stomach for no reason became swollen and painful. Every night the swollen stomach would be shaking and something would be moving inside it. Several visits to hospitals yielded no result. When I came to the Faith Clinic, I completed the basic ministration procedures and began the follow up ministration. I vomited so many things during this period and surprisingly before the 4th week of the follow up ministration the swelling and accompanying pain was gone. Another testimony is that before I came here, I used to hear a strange voice crying in my ears. Today, I do not hear any strange voice and I am completely free. I give all the glory to God.

ANCIENT CURSE OF LIMITATION BROKEN

Many years ago in my family a man was murdered, and before he gave up the ghost he cursed my family that our male children would not see their fortieth birthday. In one day, ten men in their thirties died in our larger family. This tragedy led to the establishment of a strange altar of longevity for men, with a covenant that forbids men from owning their own buildings. After many years of observing the rules of the covenant, my father who had crossed the barrier of forty years, decided to build his own house. He completed the house but the altars struck the house with thunder and everything went up in flames. From this point nobody dared build a house in my family, until I met Bishop Chigbundu, who led me to destroy the evil altars and raise a new altar with sacrifice to God. Today, in a family where men of ninety years have no personal buildings, I own buildings in different parts of the country. Praise God! - JD

CHAPTER

6

GOD'S PROPHETIC ASSIGNMENTS FOR ALTAR VICTORIES

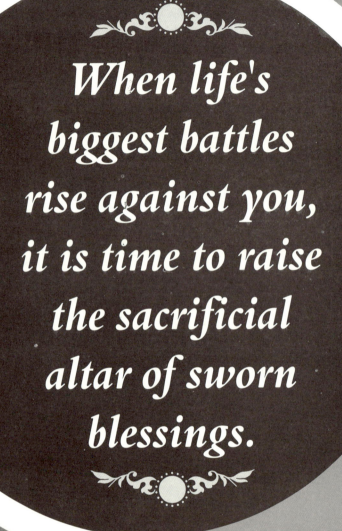

When life's biggest battles rise against you, it is time to raise the sacrificial altar of sworn blessings.

6

GOD'S PROPHETIC ASSIGNMENTS FOR ALTAR VICTORIES

"And by a prophet the Lord brought Israel out of Egypt and by a prophet was he preserved".
Hosea 12: 13

In this, I want to place in your hand a most important tool of victory in the battle of altars. This is a fundamental aspect of the war of altars, without which total triumph remains more or less a balloon dream. In my own life and ministry, I have myself been a privilege beneficiary of this mystery of God's appointed Prophet in Altar victory.

The above scripture says that God used a prophet to rescue Israel from the power of Egypt and the god of their altars of slavery. And it was through the instrumentality of the prophet that He preserved the destiny of Israel. God has not changed. He is the same yesterday, today and forever.

"I am the Lord, I change not, therefore ye sons of Jacob are not consumed". Malachi 3: 6

"Jesus Christ, the same yesterday, today and forever". Hebrews 13:8

In the wisdom of God, He ordained that victory over wicked spiritual altars will be hinged to the ministry of His anointed servants. God has raised certain vessels of deliverance in the body of Christ. To despise and disdain them is to deny oneself of the Anointing upon their lives. These are tested and proven divine agents whom God has commissioned to raise anointed ministry or church altars at His appointed locations. By their ministry, the Lord will deliver you from spiritual bondage to wicked altars that are speaking over your life, family, business etc. and it is by their ministry that you will be preserved.

You may be more educated than they are; you may be better placed in the society, you may even be riding a better car, and so on. But all that is totally irrelevant. In the final analysis, they are carrying the oil of your deliverance on their heads. It is time to locate that spiritual father or spiritual mother whom God has commissioned for your liberty over mysterious altars.

God has raised human vessels via the fivefold ministry-Apostles, Prophets, Evangelists, Pastors and Teachers. Ephesians 4:11

God has raised men throughout the Body of Christ with the anointing for deliverance. With all humility, I have seen God set people free through strange deliverances.

God has specially appointed His anointed servants to

raise divinely empowered altars of deliverance. When you locate such ministries, they become your city of refuge into which you can run to when the battle of life is hottest.

In the book of Jeremiah, God gives an explanation of how the ministry of these deliverers will function.

> *Before I formed thee in the belly I knew thee; and before thou camest forth out of the womb I sanctified thee, and I ordained thee a prophet unto the nations. See, I have this day set thee over the nations and over the kingdoms, to root out, and to pull down, and to destroy, and to throw down, to build, and to plant. Jer 1:5,10*

Jeremiah was born to be a prophet to the nations. His ministry was characterized with the pulling down of wicked kingdoms harassing God's people and also the building and planting of the destinies that had suffered strange attacks.

It was a twofold appointment.

Root out, Pull down, Destroy and Throw down all satanic systems (altars) that were in existence before he was born.

Build and plant new godly systems (altars) that will ensure fulfillment of destinies of men.

Prophetic Assignment 1

Breaking and Tearing Down of Evil Altars

And, behold, there came a man of God out of Judah by the word of the LORD unto Bethel: and Jeroboam stood by the altar to burn incense. And he cried against the altar in the word of the LORD, and said, O altar, altar, thus saith the LORD; Behold, a child shall be born unto the house of David, Josiah by name; and upon thee shall he offer the priests of the high places that burn incense upon thee, and men's bones shall be burnt upon thee. And he gave a sign the same day, saying, This is the sign which the LORD hath spoken; Behold, the altar shall be rent, and the ashes that are upon it shall be poured out. And it came to pass, when king Jeroboam heard the saying of the man of God, which had cried against the altar in Bethel, that he put forth his hand from the altar, saying, Lay hold on him. And his hand, which he put forth against him, dried up, so that he could not pull it in again to him. The altar also was rent, and the ashes poured out from the altar, according to the sign which the man of God had given by the word of the LORD.
1 Kings 13:1-5

In the above scriptures, we see how God sent His prophet on a deliverance agenda to a wicked altar that had oppressed His people. This prophet was specially equipped to pronounce divine judgement on the evil altars, and on the evil custodians of those altars.

God has not changed. Today, He has specially appointed and anointed generals in the field of breaking every altar that is claiming ownership of your destiny, your children, your career etc. In the scripture above, we see how God split the evil altar in two and poured out the ashes.

When you locate the covering of the servants of God for your life and you remain; abide and establish yourself there obeying all the instructions given to you, there will be the destruction of evil altars just like the story in the above scriptural text.

When the pastor or prophet of your deliverance commands you to pray, then pray. When he says fast, then fast. When he says serve at the altar of God, then obey. When he commands that you offer a sacrifice, obey joyfully. God does not need your money. You are the one in need of deliverance.

When God sent Prophet Elijah to the widow of Zarephath in **1 Kings 15: 5-11**, it was not so that Elijah would not die of hunger. He was sent to deliver the widow's family from starvation. God could feed the prophet without the help of any man; He fed him using the ravens which are known to be stingy birds. Do not let the devil rob you of your deliverance. Bring offerings and sacrificial seeds to the altar of your prophet. Giving into the prophet's life is the cheapest way to provoke quick release of the anointing they carry.

Many Christians have cheated themselves. They say,

"Pastor wants to eat my money". Yet they are seeking deliverance under the same pastor's ministry. How foolish! Your sworn enemies are busy servicing the wicked altars that are fighting you day and night. They are busy feeding the priests that are making daily incantations with your name and you think you will win this battle of altars while your own altar remains dry. Lack of seeds, offerings, sacrifices on your prophet's altar speaks against a person. Many Christians are their own biggest opposition. Such is an avenue by which many people are unknowingly cooperating with the enemy over their inheritances. Sow that seed into the life of that prophet fighting for your deliverance at the altar.

> "Believe the Lord your God and you shall be established. Believe also His prophets and you shall prosper". 2 Chronicles 20:20

What does this mean? Simply this: YOUR PROPHET IS FOR YOUR PROFIT! Is it possible for one to encounter profiting without an initial investment?
God has raised that man to breakdown the evil altars. Rejoice in this truth and take responsibility.

Prophetic Assignment 2

Repairing and Building up God's Altars

> And Elijah said unto all the people, Come near unto me. And all the people came near unto him. And he repaired the altar of the LORD that was broken down. And Elijah took twelve stones,

according to the number of the tribes of the sons of Jacob, unto whom the word of the LORD came, saying, Israel shall be thy name: And with the stones he built an altar in the name of the LORD: and he made a trench about the altar, as great as would contain two measures of seed. And he put the wood in order, and cut the bullock in pieces, and laid him on the wood, and said, Fill four barrels with water, and pour it on the burnt sacrifice, and on the wood. And he said, Do it the second time. And they did it the second time. And he said, Do it the third time. And they did it the third time. And the water ran round about the altar; and he filled the trench also with water. And it came to pass at the time of the offering of the evening sacrifice, that Elijah the prophet came near, and said, LORD God of Abraham, Isaac, and of Israel, let it be known this day that thou art God in Israel, and that I am thy servant, and that I have done all these things at thy word. Hear me, O LORD, hear me, that this people may know that thou art the LORD God, and that thou hast turned their heart back again. Then the fire of the LORD fell, and consumed the burnt sacrifice, and the wood, and the stones, and the dust, and licked up the water that was in the trench. And when all the people saw it, they fell on their faces: and they said, The LORD, he is the God; the LORD, he is the God.
1 Kings 18:30-39

In the above scripture, we see another spiritual operation of the ministry of prophets of God; to repair God's altars in the lives and destinies of the saints. Only when the altars of God are repaired and built can you see the fire of God fall in your favour. Prophet Elijah did not call fire from heaven without first repairing the broken altar in Israel.

God has sent some anointed prophets today with a special assignment of repairing the broken spiritual foundations of the saints by recovering lost glories and rebuilding the destinies that have been torn down by the enemy's altar. By aligning yourself with their ministry and cooperating with them, you position your life for divine repair and restoration. You gain lost blessings, lost opportunities, lost benefits in supernatural ways. Prophets do not need you rather you need them. You need what they are carrying. They are the vessels of God's restoration agenda.

God sent them to walk alongside you as you build. They are helpers of destiny. God will not jump down from heaven. He has already placed His messenger around your life, with a deliverance anointing to repair what was once broken down or destroyed.

> *Then the prophets, Haggai the prophet, and Zechariah the son of Iddo, prophesied unto the Jews that were in Judah and Jerusalem in the name of the God of Israel, even unto them. Then rose up Zerubbabel the son of Shealtiel, and Jeshua the son of Jozadak, and began to build the house of God which is at Jerusalem: and with them were the prophets of God helping them. Ezra 5:1-2*

God has sent them to help you in the rebuilding and repair process. Take full advantage of their grace. Do not join others to mock them or fight them. There is a "Touch Not" prophetic unction on their foreheads.

> *He suffered no man to do them wrong: yea, he reproved kings for their sakes; Saying, Touch not mine anointed, and do my prophets no harm.*
> *Ps 105:14-15*

If you are around an anointed vessel, and he seems to have lost honour or value in your eyes, instead of rising up against him or joining others to negatively criticize and analyze him, please spare your life and peacefully exit his territory. For no man will touch the anointed and be guiltless.

God has sent them to repair, restore and rebuild. Hold them in high esteem. Respect the Prophet of your deliverance. Beautify his life and you will see the repairing and restoring of God's Altar of Blessing upon your life, family and destiny.

CHAPTER

7

REQUIREMENTS FOR WINNING THE BATTLE OF THE ALTARS

Whatever you see as the operations of the negative altar is a counterfeit of what is obtainable on the Altar of God.

7

REQUIREMENTS FOR WINNING THE BATTLE OF THE ALTARS

To win the battle of altars, there are basic steps and principles you must follow and employ to enjoy continual victory.

Be Born Again

> *Jesus answered and said unto him, Verily, verily, I say unto thee, Except a man be born again, he cannot see the kingdom of God. Nicodemus saith unto him, How can a man be born when he is old? can he enter the second time into his mother's womb, and be born? Jesus answered, Verily, verily, I say unto thee, Except a man be born of water and of the Spirit, he cannot enter into the kingdom of God. That which is born of the flesh is flesh; and that which is born of the Spirit is spirit. John 3:3-6*

Victory in the battle of altars begins at giving your life to Jesus Christ by accepting Him as your Personal Lord and Saviour. This is the foundation of your victory and deliverance. If you have not yet given your heart to the Lord, please it would do you great gain to do so today.

There is no promise of victory for the unsaved sinner. Jesus purchased our redemption and deliverance on the Cross of Calvary. Calvary is the Highest Altar God ever raised on earth. To reject the sacrifice of Jesus at Calvary's altar is to sign up for a lifetime of victimization at the altars of the wicked one and then ultimately end up in hell, the place of everlasting torment. Position yourself for victory. The Cross is the place of power. Surrender it all at the Cross.

Receive the Baptism of the Holy Spirit

> *But ye shall receive power, after that the Holy Ghost is come upon you: and ye shall be witnesses unto me both in Jerusalem, and in all Judaea, and in Samaria, and unto the uttermost part of the earth. Acts 1:8*

The baptism of the Holy Spirit is God's empowerment operation for all believers. Do not belittle this great experience. It is God's secret weapon in the hands of the children of God enabling him with raw power. The baptism of the Holy Spirit is God's special initiation into the realms of fire and power. Jesus is the baptizer of men. Ask Him to fill you with His Holy Spirit. This will make all the difference. Go to a Holy Ghost tongues speaking church. Those who mock this experience do so at their own peril.

> *And when the day of Pentecost was fully come, they were all with one accord in one place. And suddenly there came a sound from heaven as of a rushing*

mighty wind, and it filled all the house where they were sitting. And there appeared unto them cloven tongues like as of fire, and it sat upon each of them. And they were all filled with the Holy Ghost, and began to speak with other tongues, as the Spirit gave them utterance. Acts 2:1-4

Lay Hold on God's Word of Deliverance

He sent his word, and healed them, and delivered them from their destructions. Ps 107:20

Search out and lay hold on what God has said in His Word about your deliverance. Maximize every opportunity that comes your way to learn more about God's victory in Christ, and about what God expects of you as a believer. It is only through the Word of God that you can gain access to insight and knowledge of your authority in Christ. A revelation of this divine authority will energize your spirit for a victorious prayer life.

SPIRITUAL WEAPONS FOR OVERCOMING THE WICKED ALTARS

There are indispensable but mysteriously effective weapons that destroys evil altars. They must go together for maximum result.

Prayer
A praying Christian is a winning Christian. A part time praying Christian will never win any battles because

there are no part time battles. Winning the battle of the altar demands that you make praying a lifestyle. Praying must become like breathing to you.

> *And he spake a parable unto them to this end, that men ought always to pray, and not to faint.*
> *Luke 18:1*

This weapon is called deliverance and spiritual warfare prayer. Deliverance and spiritual warfare prayer is not an intercessory prayer but confrontational aggressive prayer with specific areas in focus. It is a prayer where you address and destroy certain altars, spirits, deities, locations, objects and cast out all their representatives from an individual or group of persons. It is a prayer where you destroy the power of witchcraft and other spirits that operates from the altar. By this confrontational prayer, evil laws, covenants, dedications, curses and assignments are destroyed. The strongholds of the altars are pulled down.

It is important to let you know that deliverance prayer is not all that you need to obtain the result you desire. Under the anointing of the Holy Ghost, demons are bound to flee. Deliverance prayer will open a new door to you but will not take you into the house. It will stop what kept you on one spot in life but will not move you forward. Deliverance prayer will destroy what kept you unmarried but will not give you a life partner.

It will take the second weapon of sacrifice on a new altar to release the benefit of deliverance. In Judges 6:25 & 26

God showed the principles on how to deal with altars and obtain maximum results. He commanded Gideon to destroy his father's altars in verse 25 and raise a new altar with sacrifice in verse 26.

> *And it came to pass the same night, that the LORD said unto him, Take thy father's young bullock, even the second bullock of seven years old, and throw down the altar of Baal that thy father hath, and cut down the grove that is by it. And build an altar unto the LORD thy God upon the top of this rock, in the ordered place, and take the second bullock, and offer a burnt sacrifice with the wood of the grove which thou shalt cut down.*
> *Judges 6:25-26*

This action does not allow any vacuum to exist. Altars respond to altars. Sacrifice answers to sacrifice. In the spirit realm like begets like. Many people stop at deliverance ministrations without sacrifice that will silence the negative voices speaking against them from wicked altars. Sacrifice is the voice of any altar. If the voice of sacrifices of your ancestral altars denied you access to your destiny, the voice of your sacrifices on God's altar will usher you into your destiny.

Painful Sacrifice
This is the weapon many are not willing to use because of what it involves. Prayer of deliverance involves you speaking and commanding demons to go but sacrifice involves giving out something very dear to you to move to the next level.

God established the mystery of sacrifice right from the garden of Eden to the Cross to show us how to win prolonged and protracted issues in our lives.

What determines the quality of sacrifice you make is the value you place on your demand.

In John 3:16 "For God so loved the world, that he gave his only begotten Son, that whosoever believeth in him should not perish, but have everlasting life". What determined the sacrifice was God's value for humanity.

> *Jesus, when he had cried again with a loud voice, yielded up the ghost. And, behold, the veil of the temple was rent in twain from the top to the bottom; and the earth did quake, and the rocks rent; And the graves were opened; and many bodies of the saints which slept arose, And came out of the graves after his resurrection, and went into the holy city, and appeared unto many. Matt 27:50-53*

This weapon is what writes new laws on a new altar. By sacrificing Jesus, God solved the issue of sin and opened the chapter of fellowship closed against humanity through Adam and Eve once and for all. By sacrifice, we destroy old covenants and dedications and enter new covenants, dedications and establish blessings. By sacrifices, closed chapters are opened. By sacrifice, stubborn, prolonged and protracted issues are destroyed.

By sacrifice, Abraham enforced prophecy to manifest

and Isaac was born and by sacrifice, he obtained the covenant of wealth.

By sacrifice, Hannah's barrenness ended and by offering Samuel the only son she had to God, three sons and two daughters were added to her.

By sacrifice, Esther changed the death sentence against her people. By sacrifice, we silence the evil voices speaking against us. By it, we express the faith of our warfare. Unfortunately, this is the weapon many people are not prepared to engage in because it is more painful and expensive than prayer. In prayer you don't spend, rather you spend your energy while sacrifice takes something valuable from you. If we are going to succeed in dealing with altars, it is important that we follow Biblical principles.

> *The labour of the foolish wearieth every one of them, because he knoweth not how to go to the city.*
> *Eccl 10:15*

Sacrifice is the offering of something that you value most for the sake of something else you regard as more important and worthy which you desperately need. It is offering something very precious to God to obtain something very important you desire. Sacrifice is not an offering. It is not a spontaneous action. It is a premeditated action. Sacrifice is a painful offering that brings gainful result. Until something painful leaves you, something gainful will not come to you. Sacrifice is the voice and power of the altar. Sacrifice has a mysterious voice that eliminates miseries in life.

When you have done all you know how to do and there is no answer, I show you a MYSTERY and that is sacrifice. Sacrifice provokes quick response from God. God's final solution for the sin of the entire world was the sacrifice of His Son on the cross. Sacrifice is the solution for prolonged, protracted and mysterious problems of life. Sacrifice will disarm the power holding you at the junction of life. Sacrifice is an expression of your faith in the word of God. Sacrifice is a battle seed, the one stone against the Goliath of your destiny. Sacrifice takes care of your mistakes and covers your errors. Sacrifice makes up for your ignorance. Sacrifice is the weapon that stops the evil voices from strange altars speaking against you. Sacrifice is the key that unlocks the gate of your family prison.

ABRAHAM.

Abraham entered the covenant of believer's wealth by sacrifice when he offered his beloved son Isaac.

> *And the angel of the LORD called unto Abraham out of heaven the second time, And said, By myself have I sworn, saith the LORD, for because thou hast done this thing, and hast not withheld thy son, thine only son: That in blessing I will bless thee, and in multiplying I will multiply thy seed as the stars of the heaven, and as the sand which is upon the sea shore; and thy seed shall possess the gate of his enemies; And in thy seed shall all the nations of the earth be blessed; because thou hast obeyed my voice. Gen.22:15-18*

DAVID

David ended the plague that killed 70,000 men of his people by sacrifice. By sacrifice, David made God to change his mind. If God can honor David's sacrifice and stop the plague, He has not changed, He will honor your sacrifice and stop this plague ravaging your family. Take advantage of this mystery NOW.

> *So the LORD sent a pestilence upon Israel from the morning even to the time appointed: and there died of the people from Dan even to Beer-sheba seventy thousand men. And when the angel stretched out his hand upon Jerusalem to destroy it, the LORD repented him of the evil, and said to the angel that destroyed the people, It is enough: stay now thine hand. And the angel of the LORD was by the threshing place of Araunah the Jebusite. And David spake unto the LORD when he saw the angel that smote the people, and said, Lo, I have sinned, and I have done wickedly: but these sheep, what have they done? let thine hand, I pray thee, be against me, and against my father's house. And Gad came that day to David, and said unto him, Go up, rear an altar unto the LORD in the threshing floor of Araunah the Jebusite. And David, according to the saying of Gad, went up as the LORD commanded. And Araunah looked, and saw the king and his servants coming on toward him: and Araunah went out, and bowed himself before the king on his face upon the ground. And Araunah said, Wherefore is my lord the king*

come to his servant? And David said, To buy the threshing floor of thee, to build an altar unto the LORD, that the plague may be stayed from the people. And Araunah said unto David, Let my lord the king take and offer up what seemeth good unto him: behold, here be oxen for burnt sacrifice, and threshing instruments and other instruments of the oxen for wood. All these things did Araunah, as a king, give unto the king. And Araunah said unto the king, The LORD thy God accept thee. And the king said unto Araunah, Nay; but I will surely buy it of thee at a price: neither will I offer burnt offerings unto the LORD my God of that which doth cost me nothing. So David bought the threshing floor and the oxen for fifty shekels of silver. And David built there an altar unto the LORD, and offered burnt offerings and peace offerings. So the LORD was intreated for the land, and the plague was stayed from Israel. 2 Sam 24: 15-25

THE KING OF MOAB 2 Kings 3:1-27

The king of Moab stopped the war against him by sacrifice. This heathen king and his people came under divine judgement and lost all the mighty men of war they had. When the king saw that he was about to lose everything, he resorted to the mystery of sacrifice to save the remnant of his people. He sacrificed his eldest son, the crown prince on the altar to avert total destruction. Israel who was under divine instruction to destroy everything in Moab, turned back and that was the end of the war. Though this is not a good example but the principle worked.

GIDEON Judges 6:25-35

Gideon became a judge in his nation by sacrifice. His father's altar denied him access to the throne. He was like any other poor child in his father's house even though he was destined by God to be a judge in Israel. He was ignorant of the source of his limitations and frustrations until the night God showed him what stagnated him in life. Deliverance is a product of knowledge. *"My people are destroyed for lack of knowledge" (Hosea 4:6) Jesus said "And ye shall know the truth and the truth shall make you free" (John 8:32)* You cannot confront what you have not identified. Discovery is the key to recovery. Gideon took the bull by the horn that night and destroyed the altars of his father that denied him access to his destiny. He took the next step and raised his own altar with a sacrifice. He stepped into his destiny by the voice of his sacrifice. His voice was heard by his generation. His helpers came from all directions. A nonentity suddenly became a leader of a chosen nation. The least from a poor family in Manasseh became a ruler of his people. This is the power of deliverance and sacrifice.

THE HEBREWS Exodus.12:1-14

The Hebrews ended the 430 years of bondage in Egypt

by sacrifice. What different signs and wonders performed by Moses could not achieve in years, sacrifice accomplished in one night. Pharaoh who would not bow or bend under divine judgement against them surrendered by the forces of sacrifices of the Hebrews and released them to go with stupendous wealth.

ELIJAH 1 Kings 18:30-39

Elijah ended the challenge and controversy of his life by sacrifice. The sacrifice was not the cows but a very scarce commodity in the land. Water! There was no water in the land but that was what Elijah offered to God and the fire came down. Sacrifice that will bring a miracle must cost you something. It must not be the common thing everybody offers.

HANNAH 1Sam 1:1-20

Hannah ended her barrenness by sacrifice. She had suffered so much mockery and humiliation in the hand of her mate Peninnah. She had been to Shiloh yearly with her husband to worship but never took advantage of the sacrifice on God's altar at Shiloh. Ignorance of God's provision will deny you access to them.

SOLOMON

Solomon attracted God's attention by sacrifice.

Solomon offered what his father could not offer to attract God's attention.

> *And the king went to Gibeon to sacrifice there; for that was the great high place: a thousand burnt offerings did Solomon offer upon that altar. In Gibeon the LORD appeared to Solomon in a dream by night: and God said, Ask what I shall give thee. 1 Kings 3:4-5*

The sacrifices of the past generation has kept you in the situation you found yourself, it will take your own sacrifice to move you from there to where you want to be. Too many voices from your ancestral altars are speaking against you. You must take action to stop them by producing a new voice through your own sacrifice. If it is a blood related matter, it will require blood to solve it. The journey into Egypt was by blood covenant between God and Abraham and it took the blood of a lamb to bring them out.

The mystery of altars functions on the bases of sacrifices. The wicked never raise their wicked altars without a sacrifice to match. The devil is a counterfeiting agent. Every trick he employs in the scheming of his devices are stolen principles of how God's kingdom operates.

The altar of the church may not recognize your voice for deliverance because your seed has not been registered at that altar. How can you win battles when you do not believe in giving of offering, sacrifices and tithes? Your stinginess is not denying God; rather, it is denying you and postdating the day of your total deliverance. How long do you want to wait? A major sacrificial seed on the altar can determine a radical release of generational blessings from God. Abraham obeyed God to lay his Isaac on the altar of sacrifice. This established the trans-generational blessings which today's nation of Israel enjoys.

Today's nation of Israel is small, yet it is feared globally. Somebody secured the fearful blessing of God upon Israel- Father Abraham. You too can set in motion a generational blessing for your descendants by bringing a special sacrifice to the altar of God. That is how you win the battles of Altars.

Fasting: Fasting is a weapon in the hands of the believer. Fasting, the spiritual discipline of your appetite for food, sex, etc., for an allotted time frame, is a divine instruction given to empower your spirit. Jesus said "this kind" will not go out except by fasting and praying. Some devils will behave stubborn particularly those that have supervised destructive altars in a family for generations. It is time to engage in fasting regimen to receive victory. Do not leave that trouble you are facing to chance or go away on its own. It would not. Engage in a fast. Fasting releases angels (*Matthew 4:1-11*). Fasting is the key to breaking every yoke of the wicked altars

> *Is not this the fast that I have chosen? to loose the bands of wickedness, to undo the heavy burdens, and to let the oppressed go free, and that ye break every yoke? Isaiah 58:6*

Fasting was the tool of power that Daniel used to break the power of the wicked spirit ruler of Persia (*Daniel 10:1-14*). Jesus began His Ministry with fasting; you can only begin a new season in your life by fasting your way into that new season. It still works today.

Engage the Name of Jesus *Mark 16:17*

The name of Jesus is the producer of signs in the life of the believer. It is the highest privilege given by God to all saints in the kingdom. Only through faith in the name of Jesus can we gain absolute victory in the battle of altars (*Acts 4:16*). The name of Jesus gives you unlimited authority in three worlds as seen in *Philippians 2: 5-10* Through the name of Jesus, we have divine authority in heaven, on earth and underneath the earth (the kingdom of darkness). Declare the name of Jesus with boldness and reverence in warfare prayers.

Deploy the Blood of Jesus *Revelation 12:11*

The blood of Jesus is the overcomer's battle axe. Use the declaration of the Blood of Jesus against the evil altars and their priests. Wage Blood warfare. Why use the Blood? Because the Blood of Jesus is on the Heavenly Altar above, poured out by Jesus Christ, our very own High Priest after the order of Melchizedek. *(Hebrews 9:14-11, 6:19-20)*

Make Enquiries Jeremiah 33:3

The Bible says *"Call unto me"*. That means there are many things God may not tell you unless you inquire specifically of Him. Do not merely pray scattered prayers. God loves believers who ask intelligent questions. David inquired also.

> *Therefore David inquired of the LORD, saying, Shall I go and smite these Philistines? And the LORD said unto David, Go, and smite the Philistines, and save Keilah. 1 Sam 23:2*

For example, "Lord, what is the origin of these troubles I am currently facing? Father, which specific evil power or altar is waging war against my progress? Father, who exactly is responsible for this unending marital delay? And so on.

Do not just say "Father, do it for me!" That is not an enquiry. An enquiry is a question. God answers questions. In Jeremiah 33:3, He said "Call unto me and I will ANSWER...". Spiritual babies merely cry for deliverance but spiritual adults take it a step further by asking specifically and diligently to know the root cause of the matter. Do this for some days and you will be surprised at the answer. During the days of enquiry, watch out for outstanding dreams, visions/ revelations you may receive. You may add a fasting schedule with this. Watch out for the divine awareness that comes during or after the enquiry. When God reveals that which was hidden, you cannot pretend not to know. You may also carry along your pastor or trusted spiritual friend or a partner who is accountable if you feel led to do so. Be sure to seek pastoral counseling to fully understand what God is revealing.

Remain in the Fellowship of the Church *Hebrews 12: 24-29*

The New Testament Zion is the fellowship of the saints of God. This is where the Presence of God, the Blood and the innumerable company of God's angels are positioned on standby to enforce your deliverance. When you appear regularly in Zion, i.e. church fellowship, you become a candidate for the God that functions as a consuming fire. He will consume all strange yokes of evil altars in your life. Do not forsake the assembly of the saints. You do not know the day of your visitation. *Hebrews 10:25*

Luke 19: 44. Do not miss God's visitation to His people. Zion is where the brethren gather. It is the appointed location where God keeps His appointment to deliver His people. *Obadiah 1: 17.* Deliverance is in the Church.

Church fellowship is the place where God commands His blessings upon His people. Sitting at home when you should be in church is a proof of spiritual foolishness and backsliding. Some people say "the church is in the mind, I do not have to go to church". How is that? Why do you not stay at home from Monday to Friday while expecting a salary and simply say "Work is in my mind".

God is waiting for you in church. Your greatest divine encounters are in Zion, where the saints are gathered to worship God. The blessing is commanded in Zion.

Make Bold Declarations Quiet Christians entertain noisy devils. *Acts 14:3, 1 Samuel 17: 43-51*

A Christian can only win altar battles if he is determined to keep declaring victory. You must exercise "the shout of the king". In the battle of David and Goliath, notice that both men were making bold statements according to the altars they believed in. Goliath cursed David by the gods of the Philistines and David cursed the head of Goliath by the name of the God of the covenant of circumcision i.e. the covenant God began on Abraham's altar. If David had kept quiet when Goliath spoke, it would have been a tragic story. God honoured David's declaration. *Isaiah 44: 26* Sacrificial Giving

The mystery of altars functions on the bases of sacrifices. The wicked never raise their wicked altars without a sacrifice to match. The devil is a counterfeiting agent. Every trick he employs in the scheming of his devices are stolen principles of how God's kingdom operates.

The altar of the church may not recognize your voice for deliverance because your seed has not been registered at that altar. How can you win battles when you do not believe in giving of offering, sacrifices and tithes? Your stinginess is not denying God; rather, it is denying you and postdating the day of your total deliverance. How long do you want to wait? A major sacrificial seed on the altar can determine a radical release of generational blessings from God. Abraham obeyed God to lay his Isaac on the altar of sacrifice. This established the trans-generational blessings which today's nation of Israel enjoys. Genesis 22:1-3.Genesis 9:18

Today's nation of Israel is small, yet it is feared globally. Somebody secured the fearful blessing of God upon Israel- Father Abraham.

You too can set in motion a generational blessing for your descendants by bringing a special sacrifice to the altar of God. That is how you win the battles of Altars.

> *That confirmeth the word of his servant, and performeth the counsel of his messengers; that saith to Jerusalem, Thou shalt be inhabited; and to the cities of Judah, Ye shall be built, and I will raise up the decayed places thereof. Isa 44:26*

PRACTICAL STEPS TO VICTORY

God wants you to share a testimony of total victory over evil altars that are fighting you. To lay hold of this desired victory, you may need to take the following practical steps:

Research and Study the History of Your Family and the Family of your In-laws if you are married

Ensure you ask vital questions. Which altars are or were visited by your fathers, mothers and even as far as your forefathers? Did your ancestors swear any allegiance to the idols of any altar? What covenant did I meet on ground when I was born? Are there any family patterns that I have so far ignored?

Take quality time to observe the prevailing trend of your family and your in-law's' bloodline. For singles, you may want to ask yourself, "By choosing to marry this person, am I ready to fight the battles in his/her family tree? Am I about to inherit something I am unaware of? This plague of poverty; what is the source in our family? Who did this to me? Whom am I taking after with this behaviour of shame?

Deliberately Declare War and Fight Back

To be lenient with the wicked altars speaking against your happiness is to walk on hot coals without shoes. Leave nothing to chance. Become aggressive in faith as you open fire in prayers. Fight to the point of claiming victory in this matter. Pick up your swords and battle axe. Do not spare the enemy!

Be Sensitive to Divine Revelations

Not all dreams are mere empty dreams. In a season of intense and extensive spiritual warfare prayers, have the wisdom to study the special dreams that come your way. *Job 33:14*

God may have been saying something to you but you

may have been spiritually careless, distracted or too preoccupied with the cares of this world to pay close attention to what is being said or revealed to you. He may have been trying hard to get your attention during the day, which was why He had to send a symbolic dream to you at night.

Live A Holy Life

A holy life is an asset on the battlefield of altars. Sin makes you open to unending attacks. Sin will rubbish all your efforts to win spiritual battles. Determine to live in the victory of the Cross of Jesus. Hide God's Word in your heart that you might not sin. *Psalm 119:11.* You cannot try to defeat the devil and still be a partaker of meat from his pot of sin. Your victory cannot wait. Now is the time for your deliverance. If you must secure total victory, sin should not and must not have dominion over you. *Romans 6:14*

FINAL
WORD

The devil does not fight someone whose life is not important.

FINAL WORD

God's call to do battle at the altar is a call to gain guaranteed victory. Our God is He who equips our hands to war and our fingers to fight. ***Psalm 144:1***

God is inviting you to come up hither. You cannot win invisible battles hanging around low places. This book in your hand is a call from God to you. He is commanding you to leave civilian matters and join the Army of Jesus- an Army of valiant warriors of righteousness. ***1 Timothy 4:2***

Lasting testimonies usually do not come without a fight. The beauty of it is that you are fighting from a standpoint of victory in Christ Jesus. The devil does not fight someone whose life is not important. You are facing that stiff opposition now simply because satan believes in you. Your enemy is afraid of your prophesy.

> *And from the days of John the Baptist until now the kingdom of heaven suffereth violence, and the violent take it by force. Matt 11:12*

Only by spiritual violence can you take your share of kingdom victories over the forces of mysterious altars that are waging war against your desired progress. Arise O child of Zion, deliverance is your portion!

> But upon mount Zion shall be deliverance and there shall be holiness; and the house of Jacob shall possess their possessions". Obadiah 17

Declare war with the prayer section of this book for the next 7days. Follow the instructions on self ministrations

CONFESSIONAL/ DELIVERANCE WARFARE PRAYER SECTION

Friend, now that you have discovered what is wrong with you, I would like you to pray the following deliverance prayers with holy anger against satan – he is a thief (John 10:10) and your arch – enemy. As you do, I join my faith with yours to demand answers from Heaven in Jesus mighty name. Amen!

BREAKING OF EVIL ALTARS

1. Altars by the gate of my village, break by fire in Jesus' name.

2. Altars by our village shrine, scatter by fire in Jesus' name.

3. Altars connected to trees in my village, catch fire in Jesus' name.

4. Altars connected to the rivers and lakes in my village, break in Jesus' name.

5. Altars on my family shrine, break in the mighty name

of Jesus.

6. Altars connected to my umbilical cord, be consumed by fire in Jesus' name.

7. Altars connected to my name, catch fire in Jesus' mighty name.

8. Altars that forbid consistent progress in my family, catch fire in Jesus' name.

9. Altars against the progress of first sons and daughters, break by fire in Jesus' mighty name.

10. Altars against financial progress of first sons and daughters scatter by fire in the mighty name of Jesus.

11. Altars against the marriages of first sons and daughters, scatter by fire, in the mighty name of Jesus.

12. Altars against the progress of last sons and daughters, be destroyed by fire in the name of Jesus.

13. Altars connected to my blood line (father/ mother), I break your dominion over my life in Jesus' name.

14. Altars of stagnancy, I break you by the fire of the Holy Ghost in the name of Jesus.

15. Altars connected to the moon, I scatter your influence over my life by the fire of the Holy Ghost

in Jesus' name.

16. Altars connected to the stars over my destiny, receive fire in Jesus' name.

17. Altars connected to the sun controlling my destiny, scatter by fire in Jesus' name.

18. Altars connected to the wind to distract my destiny helpers from locating me, scatter by the fire of the Holy Ghost in Jesus' name.

19. Altars connected to rocks and stones, break by fire in Jesus mighty name.

20. Altars connected to evil birds speaking against my life, break in the mighty name of Jesus.

21. Altars connected to evil animals, scatter by fire in Jesus' name.

22. Altars connected to the food my tribe forbids, break in Jesus' name.

23. Altars connected to demonic cultural rites and practices in my village working against my life, scatter in Jesus' name.

24. Altars sponsoring financial limitation in my life, break in Jesus' name.

25. Altars sponsoring failure in my life, I break you by

fire in Jesus' name.

26. Altars sponsoring limitation in my life endeavors, catch fire in Jesus' mighty name.

27. Altars sponsoring business losses, catch fire in Jesus' mighty name.

28. Altars sponsoring business stagnation, expire by the fire of the Holy Ghost in Jesus' name.

29. Altars sponsoring evil pattern in my family, scatter by fire in the mighty name of Jesus.

30. Altars sponsoring patterns of untimely death in my family, break in the name of Jesus.

31. Altars sponsoring untimely death of the progressive sons and daughters of my family, I destroy you by thunder in Jesus' name.

32. Altars sponsoring patterns of sickness in my family, I break you by fire in Jesus' name.

33. Altars sponsoring poverty at old age, receive fire in Jesus' name.

34. Altars sponsoring late marriages in my family, break by fire in Jesus' name.

35. Altars sponsoring chronic singlehood in my family, catch fire now in the powerful name of Jesus.

36. Altars sponsoring death of intelligent children in my family, scatter by Holy Ghost fire in the mighty name of Jesus.

37. Altars sponsoring evil veil over my star, break by fire in Jesus' name.

38. Altars sponsoring blackmails against me, catch fire in Jesus' name.

39. Altars sponsoring forgetfulness in the hearts of my helpers, catch fire in Jesus' name.

40. Altars of disharmony and confusion in my family, break in Jesus' name.

41. Altars that destroy good opportunities that are coming to me, break by fire in Jesus' name.

42. Altars raised on the day I was born, break by fire in Jesus' name.

43. Altars connected to the market day I was born, the thunder of God locate and break you now in Jesus' mighty name.

44. Altars that scatter the labour of my hands, expire by the fire of the Holy Ghost in Jesus' name.

45. Altars sponsoring struggle and hardship in life, break by thunder in Jesus' name.

46. Altars from the places I went to for help hindering my progress in life, receive fire now in Jesus' mighty name.

47. Altars raised through sexual immoralities hindering my marital settlement and progress, break in Jesus' name.

48. Altars raised through circumcision, expire in Jesus' name.

49. Altars established through sacrifices at various junction, receive fire in Jesus' name.

50. Altars in the street where I live, break in Jesus' name.

51. Altars in the place where I work, scatter by fire in Jesus' name.

52. Altars in the place where I do my business expire, in Jesus' name.

53. Altars in the city, town or village where I live break in Jesus' name.

54. Altars connected to snakes, catch fire in Jesus' mighty name.

55. Altars connected to the totem of my village/ family, scatter by fire in Jesus' mighty name.

56. Altars that limit educational lifting in my life catch fire now, in Jesus' name.

57. Altars that limit professional lifting in my life break from my life in Jesus' name.

58. Altars that limit my spiritual lifting, scatter by fire in Jesus' name.

59. Altars sponsoring quarrel and confusion in my marriage, catch fire in Jesus' name.

60. Altars sponsoring sickness in my body, scatter by fire in Jesus' name.

61. Altars raised with my hair and finger nails, break in Jesus' name.

62. Altars raised with my blood, scatter in Jesus' powerful name.

63. Altars with ancient money like cowries and manilas representing my money, catch fire in Jesus' name.

64. Altars raised by native doctors with salt against my destiny, scatter by fire in Jesus' name.

65. Altars raised by native doctors with sand against me, scatter by fire in Jesus' name.

66. Altars raised by native doctors with my picture, catch fire in the mighty name of Jesus.

67. Altars raised by native doctors with snail and tortoise to slow down progress in my life, scatter by thunder

in Jesus' name.

68. Altars raised against me by native doctors with powder and native chalk, scatter by fire in Jesus' name.

69. Altars raised by occult power using enchantment and curses against me, break in Jesus' name.

70. Altars of Ogun, Eziza, Olokun, Orunmila, Sango, Amadioha, Ahanjoku, Igbe, (mention the gods in your community) scatter by the Holy Ghost fire in Jesus' name.

71. Altars of servitude in my family/village, break in Jesus' name.

72. By the anointing of the Holy Ghost, I deploy the blood of Jesus against representatives of evil altars in my life. I command them to come out by air or liquid through my mouth and other openings of my body, in Jesus' mighty name.

SILENCING THE VOICE OF EVIL SACRIFICES

1. Evil sacrifices speaking against my destiny, be silent forever in Jesus' name.

2. I silence the voice of evil sacrifices speaking failure

into my life in Jesus' name.

3. By the power in the blood of Jesus, I silence the voices of evil sacrifices speaking sickness into my body in Jesus' mighty name.

4. You voice of evil sacrifices speaking limitations into my life, be silent in Jesus' name.

5. By thunder and fire, I destroy the power of evil sacrifices speaking disapproval in the hearts of my destiny helpers in Jesus' name.

6. Evil sacrifices speaking delays in my life, be silent forever in Jesus' name.

7. I deploy the power in the blood of Jesus to silence the voice of evil sacrifices speaking stagnancy into my life in Jesus' name.

8. Evil sacrifices speaking poverty into my life be silent forever in Jesus' name.

9. I silence the voice of evil sacrifices speaking hardship and struggle into my life in Jesus' name.

10. By the power in the blood of Jesus, I silence the voice of evil sacrifices speaking financial hardship and limitation into my life in Jesus' name.

11. I destroy the voices of evil sacrifices speaking failure and stagnation into my business in Jesus' name.

12. I silence the voices of evil sacrifices speaking against my academic and professional progress in Jesus' name.

13. You evil voice from strong sacrifices speaking against my marriage and home be silenced forever in Jesus' mighty name.

14. Evil sacrifices speaking against my ministry, church growth and expansion, be silent forever in Jesus' name.

15. I deploy the blood of Jesus against every evil sacrifices speaking against my progress, greatness and lifting in Jesus' name.

16. You wicked voices from my family altar, speak no more in Jesus' name.

17. You wicked voice from my father's altars, be silent forever in Jesus' name.

18. You strange voice from my mother's altars speak no more in Jesus' name.

19. You evil voice speaking from my village altars against my destiny, be silent forever in Jesus' name.

20. All deposits representing voices from wicked altars, I command you to come out of me by air or liquid through my mouth and nose in Jesus' name.

OTHER BOOKS BY
Bishop Abraham
CHIGBUNDU

- Voice of Freedom (Daily Devotional)
- Loose Him and Let Him Go
- I Believe in Deliverance
- Wicked Times and Seasons
- Witchcraft Manipulations Exposed
- Achievers Secrets
- Developing Another Spirit
- Discover to Recover
- Changing Wicked Times and Seasons'
- From Story to Glory
- Learning in the School of Marriage
- Altar versus Altars
- Spiritual Checkpoint
- Destined for Greatness but Tied
- 30 Secrets of Success
- How to Open Closed Human Destinies
- Overcoming Evil Waters
- Life Transforming Words of Bishop Abraham Chigbundu
- 7 Things God does not Know
- Abiding in His Presence

DR. ABRAHAM
CHIGBUNDU

BREAKING
FAULTY FAMILY
FOUNDATIONS

TO PURCHASE BISHOP CHIGBUNDU'S BOOKS
VISIT WWW.AMAZON.COM

30 SECRETS OF SUCCESS

DR ABRAHAM CHIGBUNDU

Altar
Versus
Altars

Deliverance By Sacrifice

Dr. Abraham Chigbundu

To purchase **Bishop Chigbundu's Books**
visit www.amazon.com

CHANGING WICKED TIMES & SEASONS

TIMES & SEASONS

DR ABRAHAM CHIGBUNDU

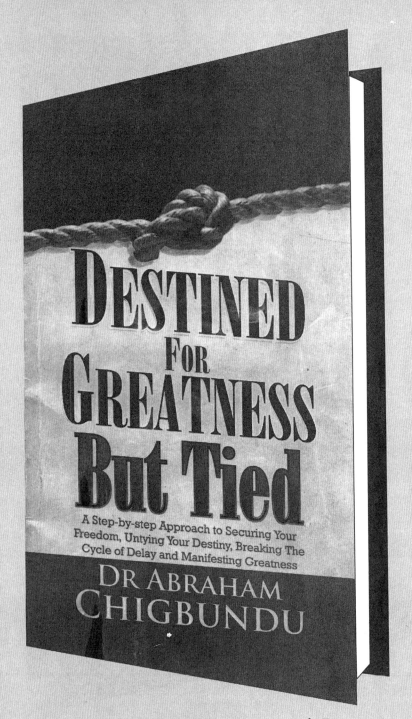

DESTINED FOR GREATNESS But Tied

A Step-by-step Approach to Securing Your Freedom, Untying Your Destiny, Breaking The Cycle of Delay and Manifesting Greatness

DR ABRAHAM CHIGBUNDU